To Adeline

— on a delightful evening with Bales

[signature]

Choose Life

CHOOSE LIFE

Bernard Mandelbaum

Random House · *New York*

1-18-80

First Printing

Copyright © 1968 by Bernard Mandelbaum

Library of Congress Catalog Card Number: 67-22659

Manufactured in the United States of America

Calligraphy by Alan Zwiebo

Acknowledgment is hereby made to the following for permission to reprint from their works:

Association Press for *The Meaning of Service* by Harry Emerson Fosdick.

Behrman House, Inc., for *Sayings of the Fathers*, translated by Joseph H. Hertz.

The Belknap Press of Harvard University Press for *The Occasional Speeches of Justice Oliver Wendell Holmes*, compiled by Mark DeWolfe Howe.

A. C. Black Ltd., London, and The Macmillan Company for *Philosophy of Civilization* by Albert Schweitzer.

Bloch Publishing Co. for *Rabbi Israel Salanter* by Menahem G. Glenn.

The Burning Bush Press for *Past and Present: Selected Essays* by Israel Friedlaender. Copyright © 1961 by The Burning Bush Press, New York.

The Burning Bush Press for *Seminary Addresses and Other Papers* by Solomon Schechter. Copyright © 1959 by The Burning Bush Press, New York.

The Clarendon Press, Oxford, for *The Works of Aristotle—Ethica Nichomacea* from Vol. IX, edited and translated by W. D. Ross.

Collins-Knowlton-Wing, Inc. for "It's Time to Close Our Carnival" by Sloan Wilson. Copyright © 1958 by Time, Inc.

Columbia University Press for *The World of the Four Freedoms* by Sumner Welles. Copyright 1943 by Columbia University Press.

Committee for Economic Development for "Paying for Better Public Schools," New York, December 1959.

Conference on Science, Philosophy and Religion in Their Relation to the Demo-

Harper & Row, Publishers, Inc. for *Judaism and Modern Man* by Will Herberg. Copyright 1951 by Will Herberg.

Harper & Row, Publishers, Inc. for *On Active Service in Peace and War* by Henry L. Stimson.

Harper & Row, Publishers, Inc. for *Self-Renewal: The Individual and the Innovative Society* by John W. Gardner.

Holt, Rinehart and Winston, Inc. and Routledge & Kegan Paul Ltd. for *Escape from Freedom* by Erich Fromm. Copyright 1941 by Erich Fromm.

Holt, Rinehart and Winston, Inc. and William Heinemann Ltd. for *The Gates of the Forest* by Elie Wiesel.

Holt, Rinehart and Winston, Inc. for *Justice and Mercy* by Max Arzt. Copyright © 1963 by Max Arzt.

Holt, Rinehart and Winston, Inc. for *Man for Himself* by Erich Fromm.

Holt, Rinehart and Winston, Inc. for "Speech to Those Who Say Comrade" from *Public Speech* by Archibald MacLeish. Copyright 1936, © 1964 by Archibald MacLeish.

Horovitz Publishing Co. Ltd. for *Philosophia Judaica:* Maimonides: The Guide of the Perplexed, edited by Julius Guttman.

Houghton Mifflin Company for "A View of Oxford Mississippi" from *A Continuing Journey* by Archibald MacLeish. Copyright © 1967 by Archibald MacLeish.

The Houston Post for a column by Marguerite Johnston, January 20, 1957.

Indiana University Press for *The Moral Decision* by Edmond Cahn. Copyright © 1955 by Indiana University Press.

The Institute for Religious and Social Studies for essays by R. M. MacIver, Philip Sokol, and Jane M. Hoey in *The Assault on Poverty* and *Individual Responsibility*, edited by R. M. MacIver.

The Institute for Religious and Social Studies for "The Religion of a Scientist," an address by Arthur H. Compton delivered at the Jewish Theological Seminary of America.

The Jewish Publication Society of America for *Hebrew Ethical Wills*, edited by Israel Abrahams.

The Jewish Publication Society of America for *The Holy Scriptures*.

The Jewish Publication Society of America for *Studies in Judaism* by Solomon Schechter.

The Jewish Publication Society of America for *Students Scholars and Saints* by Louis Ginzberg.

The Jewish Theological Seminary of America for *Amos Vs. Amaziah* by Shalom Spiegel.

Edward M. Keating and *Saturday Review* for "The New Left: What Does It Mean?" September 24, 1966.

Alfred A. Knopf, Inc. and Faber and Faber Ltd. for *Markings* by Dag Hammarskjöld. Translated by Leif Sjöberg and W. H. Auden. Copyright © 1964 by Alfred A. Knopf, Inc.

Alfred A. Knopf, Inc. and Hamish Hamilton Ltd. for *The Rebel* by Albert

Schocken Books Inc. and Thames & Hudson Ltd. for *Tales of the Hasidim: The Early Masters,* edited by Martin Buber. Schocken Books, Inc. for *Tales of the Hasidim: The Later Masters,* edited by Martin Buber. Copyright 1947, 1948 by Schocken Books Inc. For *Ten Rungs: Hasidic Sayings* by Martin Buber. Copyright 1947 by Schocken Books, Inc.

Charles Scribner's Sons for *The Essays of Francis Bacon,* edited by Mary August Scott.

Charles Scribner's Sons for *Farmington* by Clarence Darrow.

Charles Scribner's Sons for *Man's Quest for God* by Abraham J. Heschel.

University of Chicago Press and Random House, Inc. for *Apocrypha,* translated by Edgar J. Goodspeed. Copyright 1938 by Edgar J. Goodspeed.

The Viking Press, Inc. for *Philosopher's Holiday* by Irwin Edman.

Yale University Press for *Psychoanalysis and Religion* by Erich Fromm.

To Judith . . .

the wisest choice of life for myself
. . . and for Joel
            Dasi
                David
                    Debra
                        Naomi

Foreword

The little girl's complete absorption with a pencil and drawing pad impressed her mother.

"What are you doing?" she asked.

"I am making a picture of God," was the answer.

"That's interesting . . . but you know, dear, no one knows *exactly* what God looks like," the mother felt compelled to comment.

"Really?" the child answered. "Well, they will know when I finish this!"

Many a truth about man and society is symbolized in this brief exchange. Just as a child expresses himself and expects answers in terms which are concrete, tangible and specific, so, too, the childish, naïve mind expects clear, precise, unequivocal evidence and portrayal of truth, goodness, righteousness, God. The mature, realistic person recognizes the realities of life's complexities—its perplexing paradoxes as well as its continuity.

To complicate matters even more, the insight of a third-century scholar, Rabbi Isaac, reveals the challenge which confronts any quest for the eternal values. "Significant experiences and genuine blessings—love, compassion, justice, brotherhood, peace—are not to be found in anything that can be measured or weighed, or counted, but in that which is hidden from the eye."

This intangible nature of the realities of life explains the method of instruction of a first - century teacher, Rabbi Hanina, the son of Dosa. He compared wisdom to a deep well of cool, sweet water. People could not enjoy its refreshing nourishment until a wise man tied one small string to another, attached it to a pitcher and then drew up water for drink. Thus, Rabbi Hanina continued, did King Solomon, in his wisdom, tie one little story, parable and metaphor to another until he probed and clarified the meaning of wisdom.

Wisdom, therefore, is best revealed for our study and guidance by illustration and vivid language which strike responsive chords in the experience of Everyman.

The Bible is one of the best-known examples of such dramatic and vivid expression of eternal truths that serve as signposts for man. This is true of Jewish thought throughout its development, just as it characterizes the literary expression of all great civilizations. Literature achieves greatness when universal truths are given concrete, meaningful and relevant formulation.

Each chapter of this volume begins with an attempt to express a value of vital human concern which was published as the High Holy Day Messages of the Jewish Theological Seminary of America. There is a reason for choosing this holiest period of the year to address a moral lesson to all mankind. According to rabbinic tradition, Adam—the father of all mankind—was born on the first day of the New Year (Rosh Hashanah). On this day, therefore, one must be concerned with the destiny of all men, regardless of religion, race, culture or nationality. The New Year, the birthday of man, symbolizes the brotherhood of all men who have one father, Adam.

The creation of Adam symbolizes other significant truths about life and the world which are stressed in the High Holy Day Messages.

The question is asked by a second-century teacher: "Why did God create a single man, Adam? In His omnipotence, the Almighty could have fashioned millions of people at once."

The answer: "This is to teach a lesson about the value and sacredness of each and every person. Just as the world originally consisted of one man, each person is as important as the universe. Therefore, he who destroys a single person destroys the world. And he who saves a single person saves the world."

In a society where most men concentrate their confidence, resources, energies and talents on the power of machines, the High Holy Day Messages seek to strengthen man's confidence in the power of his own action and decisions. The rabbis of the Mishnah stress this in still another way: "Each man," they tell us, "should look upon the world's destiny as if it is evenly balanced between forces which can destroy it, on the one side, and those which can save it, on the other. What you do, as an individual, tips the balance and either saves the world or condemns it to destruction."

There is another lesson to be derived from the creation of a single man, Adam, which explains a recurrent theme of the Messages. In a tractate of the Talmud, one of the rabbis suggests that God fashioned man from a mold which He uses each time that a person is created. This gives rise to the following question: "When man stamps out coins from a mold, each coin resembles the other. Why is it, then, that the Almighty fashions all men from the same original mold and yet no two people—not even identical twins—are exactly alike?"

To this they answer: "This is to teach a lesson. All men have a great deal in common; they derive from the same mold. Yet no two men are alike. Each person has a uniqueness and individuality that is all his own. It is man's responsibility to develop and give expression to his individuality, or the purpose of creation is defeated."

The Messages seek to portray the beauty of this diversity of individuals, historic groups, religions, nations and cultures of the One World in which we live. In probing for the universal truths that unite all men, there is always sensitivity and concern for the differences that enhance life and the world.

These emphases on the uniqueness of individuals and the influence of a person's action are fundamental to the Messages. In addition to the power of personal performance, however, thought and the power of ideas are viewed as decisive forces in shaping the character of man and society.

Surrounded as we are by "things," dependent as we are on the tangible which we seek to possess, there is the tendency to judge the nature of ideas in terms of the quality of "things." However, an eighth-century parable points out the unique attribute of ideas:

Two neighboring merchants were engaged in conversation while business was at a standstill. "Look," one said, "there are no customers today. I sell vegetables; you sell linen. Let us exchange our merchandise." This they did. Upon completing the transaction, the second merchant said: "We did something, but what did we gain? I have your things and you have mine. However, I have a suggestion that will really benefit both of us. This morning I studied a chapter of Bible and I know you studied another chapter of Bible. You teach me your chapter and I will teach you mine . . . and we will end up knowing *two* chapters each."

Ideas, in contrast to things, have an influence that is way out of proportion to their apparent size or power. They can be in many places at the same time. They have a vitality that can increase, rather than weaken, with time. Ideas are active even when men are asleep.

The Messages seek to tap the unique power of ideas as a good influence on man and the world. Especially in our day, when more and more minds are caught up in the new game of Theology and actually presume to utter the words "God is dead"—implying, as it does, a world of chance, uncertainty and unpredictability—the Messages seek to spell out the relevance and worldly wisdom of ideas which penetrate the immediate in experience and express the eternal, dependable principles of truth and moral law.

The greater part of this volume consists of selections from Jewish and world literature which augment and develop the central ideas of the High Holiday Messages. In selecting the passages, I was guided by the instruction of Rabbi Hanina, son of Dosa, always seeking the illustration, the story, the metaphor, the vivid phrase which would enable the reader to come as close as possible to "touching" and "tasting" a vital value and relevant idea for the strengthening and nourishment of his own understanding and commitment to truth and goodness.

The process by which the Messages were written is itself an illustration of the role of diversity of experience and thought in arriving at universal ideas. Mr. Victor M. Ratner is co-author of each Message in which we sought to hammer out an idea on the anvil of our own experience, guided by the insight of Jewish teaching, which speaks to all men at all times. We began more or less with the assumption that my role derives from an academic training in the history of ideas, and Mr. Ratner is an artist in the use of words. The seemingly endless dialogues that preceded the writing of each Message alerted me to the power of a well-chosen word. It became clear that one can only be an artist with words if one has ideas to express, as does Mr. Ratner. Neither one of us can determine now who is responsible for any particular idea or the way it is formulated. In expressing gratitude to him, I know that his most meaningful reward is the knowledge that his efforts may help good men everywhere derive some new insight into the meaning and purpose of their lives.

In preparing the High Holiday Messages, we had a remarkable resource of insight and learning in the scholars on the faculty and other associates at the Jewish Theological Seminary of America. Chancellor Louis Finkelstein was especially helpful at all times. A good friend, Mr. Samuel J. Levy, headed a committee which made the Messages available to readers throughout the country.

I am deeply grateful to Miss Arlene Carmen for her devotion and good judgment in supervising the preparation of the manuscript. Her careful research in tracing sources will make this volume so much more meaningful to the reader. To her assistants in this, Mrs. Irene Sirugo and Miss Shifra Tichovolsky, my gratitude.

September 1968   B. M.
Tishri 5729

Contents

1. CHOOSE LIFE

Do people think of you as being rich or poor?

And how do they measure this?

It is easy for any of us to become confused about the meanings of wealth and poverty.
We often think of wealth primarily as the piling up of money, or of the things money can buy; we measure our wealth by whether we have more or less of these things than others do.

Yet isn't this strange:

To be wealthy is to derive joy and fulfillment from what one has—*and no amount of ownership of things can insure this for us.*

On the contrary, the more things we own, the more likely we are to want more and more of them, the more likely we are to be always in want!

And isn't this also strange:

While we seek possession of things in order to live well within ourselves and with others, we see all around us that such possessions tend to splinter a man's life and separate him from others.

How, then, can we genuinely enrich ourselves?

*We can arrive at enduring achievement and our own ful-
fillment only through the wealth of life itself.*

For these choices are always open to us:

To choose *things* . . . which limit us, divide us and con-
sume us.

Or to choose *life* . . . which enlarges us, involves us and
continues us.

And this is what it means to choose life:
It means:
—gaining possession of knowledge of ourselves, our fellow-men and of the universe;
—experiencing the beauty of Creation of a tree, of the
sky, of a song;
—building the structure of our lives on the foundations of
wisdom: wisdom of the past and of the present.
                    For these enlarge us.

It means:
—giving of our thoughts, our feelings and our time . . .
giving of ourselves . . . to our children, to a wife or
husband, to a friend, a neighbor;
—meeting our deepest responsibilities in the community,
in our country, and in the brotherhood of nations;
—sharing the pain and suffering of others, knowing well
that *"they who sow in tears shall reap in joy."* (Psalms
126:5)
                    For these involve us.

It means:
—fighting an evil,
—nurturing an ideal,
—fashioning a character,
all of which extend our impact and meaning in the world
beyond our own lives, joining us with the generations
of men, as with our Maker.

For these continue us.

Having chosen life . . .

Having chosen to enlarge, involve and continue ourselves . . .

We discover the endless creativity of life, its enduring
capacity for good is this: *as we share with others the
treasures of living, we increase them for ourselves.*

> *"He is the Lord of wonders Who in His goodness
> reneweth the creation every day, continually . . ."*
> (from the daily prayer book)

These enlarge us...

Acquiring wisdom...

There are four types among those that sit in the presence of the wise: the sponge, the funnel, the strainer, and the sifter.

The sponge soaks up everything.

The funnel takes in at one ear and lets out at the other.

The strainer lets pass the wine and retains the lees.

The sifter holds back the coarse and collects the fine flour.

—ETHICS OF THE FATHERS

Wisdom begins with sacrifice of immediate pleasures for long-range purposes.

—LOUIS FINKELSTEIN

"I take the long view, the patient one, on history." . . . [The] illustration was the ancient story of The Flying Horse—of the King who sentenced a man to death. The man begged a reprieve, and obtained one by assuring the King that he'd teach His Majesty's horse to fly within a year.

The reprieve was granted, on condition that the horse be able to fly at the end of a year—or else the man be put to death. The man later explained: "Within a year, the King may die, or I may die, or the horse may die. Furthermore, in a year—who knows? Maybe the horse will learn to fly." . . . "My philosophy is like that man's. . . . Patience. I take the long-range view."

—BERNARD M. BARUCH

In addition to engineers, the world of tomorrow will also need men and women with deep roots in our moral and spiritual heritage. "It is not brains that matter most," Dostoevski once wrote, "but that which guides them—the character, the heart, the generous qualities."

Surely, it was never the Creator's design that humanity be subordinated to the machine. We cannot program a machine to know good or evil, or to be responsible for the social implications of its performance.

In the midst of vast changes imposed by technology, the student will find that one element remains unchanged—the spiritual and moral inheritance given to him by his family, his church, and his college. This is what gives purpose and meaning to his endeavors.

—DAVID SARNOFF

On your way through life you'll meet men who cling to reason, but reason gropes like a blind man with a white cane, stumbling over every pebble, and when it comes up against a wall it stops short and tries to tear it down brick by brick, quite ineffectually, because an invisible hand builds it up again, higher and thicker than ever. We, on the other hand, believe in the power of faith and ecstasy, and no wall can stand against us . . .

—ELIE WIESEL

Solomon said:
"If I ask silver and gold and precious stones and jewels, He will give them to me.
But lo, I shall ask wisdom, and all else will be included."
Therefore it is written:

"Give Thy servant therefore an understanding heart."
(I Kings 3:9)
The Holy One, blessed be He, said to him:
"Solomon, you have asked wisdom for yourself and have
not asked wealth and goods and the life of your foes;
By your life, you are now given wisdom and knowledge,
And through them I shall give you wealth and goods as well."

—MIDRASH

To remain a recipient—and be grateful. Grateful for being
allowed to listen, to observe, to understand.

—DAG HAMMARSKJÖLD

Perhaps the true societies of the mind and those one remem-
bers best are those that never meet, or that meet only once
and by accident, or that emerge suddenly in the midst of
casual conversation among a group of friends who transform
it into an exchange of ideas clearly perceived and emotions
directly felt, giving and catching mutual fire. And sometimes, when one is quite alone, one's imagination is peopled
with ideas, those one has just been reading, those to which
some reading has recently prompted one, or during or after
listening to music alone. The ultimate society of the mind,
when the spirit listeth, is a soliloquy, and that isolated heaven
is crowded with friends in the form of congenial themes.

—IRWIN EDMAN

But wisdom, where shall it be found?
And where is the place of understanding?
Man knoweth not the price thereof;
Neither is it found in the land of the living.
The deep saith: "It is not in me";
And the sea saith: "It is not with me."
It cannot be gotten for gold,
Neither shall silver be weighed for the price thereof.
It cannot be valued with the gold of Ophir,
With the precious onyx, or the sapphire.
Gold and glass cannot equal it;

Neither shall the exchange thereof be vessels of fine gold.
No mention shall be made of coral or of crystal;
Yea, the price of wisdom is above rubies.
The topaz of Ethiopia shall not equal it,
Neither shall it be valued with pure gold.
Whence then cometh wisdom?
And where is the place of understanding?

And unto man He said:
"Behold, the fear of the Lord, that is wisdom;
And to depart from evil is understanding."

—JOB 28: 12–20, 28

He maketh men to walk in Wisdom's ways;
In Suffering He lays
Foundations deep
Of Knowledge. At the heart remembered Pain,
As of a wound that bleeds, waketh in sleep.
Though we reject her, Wisdom finds a road.

—AESCHYLUS

Rabbi Yohanan, son of Zakkai, said: The wise man who fears
doing wrong is like a craftsman who has the tools of his craft
ready in his hand. The wise man who does not fear doing
wrong is like a craftsman who has no tools. And, finally, the
man who fears doing wrong but has no wisdom is like a
man who has the tools, but is no craftsman. He has the will,
but does not know what he ought to do.

—FATHERS ACCORDING TO RABBI NATHAN

To Adams, my old enemy and friend, that gnarled greatness,
    long ago.
I wrote to him, and said
That the dream of the future is better than the dream of
    the past.
Now I should hope to find the courage to say
That the dream of the future is not
Better than the fact of the past, no matter how terrible.
For without the fact of the past we cannot dream the future.

—ROBERT PENN WARREN

> Hillel said . . . the more Torah, the more life; the more
> schooling, the more wisdom; the more counsel, the more
> understanding . . .
>
> —ETHICS OF THE FATHERS

Socrates, when the young Theaetetus was introduced to him
as a lad of brilliant promise, said to him that he felt sure he
had thought a great deal. The boy answered, Oh, no—not
that, but at least he had wondered a great deal. "Ah, that
shows the lover of wisdom," Socrates said, "for wisdom
begins in wonder."

—PLATO

> Hillel said . . . "the timid cannot learn." (Ethics of the
> Fathers 2:6)
>
> . . . bashfulness is not a good thing in study. Moreover, no
> student ought to say, "How shall a fool like me ask questions
> of a very great scholar, of a brilliant sage? I have neither
> knowledge nor understanding." For if this is how he feels
> all the time, how will wisdom ever come to him? And this
> is the meaning of the maxim, "Ask like a fool and save like
> the generous." That is to say, just as the generous do not
> scatter their wealth, but also do not keep it to themselves—
> instead they give it gladly and graciously where it will do
> most good . . . so in the case of wisdom: one should engage
> in it with the proper people and at the proper time. . . .
> But a person should ask every manner of question and not
> be ashamed to do so, in order that he may learn.
>
> —RABBI JONAH

The modern sciences . . . such as anthropology, economics,
psychology, sociology, and the schools of writing which they
generate, do not treat either the past or the present with
sympathy. They bid the past stand and deliver, and bid the
public stand and swallow. They do not afford that spiritual
relief which religion and the fine arts supply, and which
humanity prizes above all else.

—JOHN JAY CHAPMAN

. . . That's one of the troubles with the world today. . . .
Everybody thinks that something should be done right away.
And that's not true. Maybe we could do with a lot of non-
doing. Maybe the thing to do now is nothing. But, you
know, the journalists and the people who, they say, control
public opinion are always calling upon something to be
done. I wish we could call a moratorium upon actions for
the next ten years; then we might be saved.

—MARK VAN DOREN

When you rise from your book, probe into what you have
learned, to discover whether there is in it anything you can
translate into reality.

—NAHMANIDES

A man of piety complained to the Baal Shem, saying: "I have
labored hard and long in the service of the Lord, and yet
I have received no improvement. I am still an ordinary and
ignorant person."

The Baal Shem answered: "You have gained the realization
that you are ordinary and ignorant, and this in itself is a
worthy accomplishment."

—HASIDIC

Leisure is a laic and secular word which points towards the
gateway of spiritual truth, much as the word "contemplation," tinged as it is with religion, points in the same direction; and both of them imply receptivity, a reliance on some
solution which shall swim into our minds without aid from
us, a half-consciousness that our own faculties are part of the
operations of Nature.

—JOHN JAY CHAPMAN

The wise in heart is called a man of discernment;
and the sweetness of the lips increaseth learning.

—PROVERBS 16:21

He [the devout man] . . . shackles the forces that crave power and strive toward superiority. . . . He gives to each of the senses that portion which is good for it. He uses his hands, his feet, and his tongue only for what is necessary, and for a good purpose. It is the same with his hearing and his sight, and the related feelings that attend them; with imagination and the power of judgment, the power to think, and memory; and with the power of will, which employs all of these others. All of these are nothing but servants, subject to the will of reason. But he does not permit one or the other of these forces and limbs to exceed in that for which it is destined, and thus to thrust back the rest.

—JUDAH HA-LEVI

. . . it seems to me that at this time we need education in the obvious more than investigation of the obscure.

—OLIVER WENDELL HOLMES

Happy is the man that findeth wisdom,
And the man that obtaineth understanding.
For the merchandise of it is better than the merchandise of
    silver,
And the gain thereof than fine gold.
She is more precious than rubies;
And all the things thou canst desire are not to be compared
    unto her.
Length of days is in her right hand;
In her left hand are riches and honor.
Her ways are ways of pleasantness,
And all her paths are peace.
She is a tree of life to them that lay hold upon her,
And happy is every one that holdeth her fast.

—PROVERBS 3:13–18

The fullness of
human experience...

Man will hereafter be called to account for depriving himself of the good things which the world lawfully allows.

—TALMUD

Quien canta, sus males espanta. (He who sings frightens away his ills.)

—MIGUEL DE CERVANTES

Rabbi Pinhas of Koretz says: "Joy is on a higher plane than grief. Even with the newborn child, tears come first and smiles only later. Joy constitutes a higher stage, for it springs from higher worlds, from the glory of God. Thus is it that joy washes away all sin."

—HASIDIC

Three things restore a man's good spirits: music, fair sights, sweet smells. Three things increase a man's self-esteem: a good home, a good wife, good clothes.

—TALMUD

A lake is the landscape's most beautiful and expressive feature. It is earth's eye.

—HENRY DAVID THOREAU

. . .

A child said *What is the grass?* fetching it to me with full
    hands;
How could I answer the child? I do not know what it is any
    more than he.
I guess it must be the flag of my disposition, out of hopeful
    green stuff woven.
Or I guess it is the handkerchief of the Lord,
A scented gift and remembrancer designedly dropt,
Bearing the owner's name someway in the corners, that we
    may see and remark, and say *Whose?*
Or I guess the grass is itself a child, the produced babe of the
    Vegetation.

. . .

—WALT WHITMAN

. . . as I read, between my eyes and book, the Moon sheds
down on harvest fields her chill of silver; I see autumnal
avenues, with the leaves falling, or swept in heaps; and storms
blow among my thoughts, with the rain beating forever on
the fields. Then Winter's upward glare of snow appears; or
the pink and delicate green of Spring in the windy sunshine;
or cornfields and green waters, and youths bathing in Summer's golden heats.

—LOGAN PEARSALL SMITH

My heart leaps up when I behold
    A rainbow in the sky:
So was it when my life began,
So is it now I am a man,
So be it when I shall grow old
    Or let me die!
The Child is father of the Man:
And I could wish my days to be
Bound each to each by natural piety.
    —WILLIAM WORDSWORTH

The heavens declare the glory of God,
And the firmament showeth His handiwork . . .
    —PSALMS 19:2

Man cannot live without placing his faith in *something* as
the source of the meaning and value of his existence, in
something that for him is absolute, ultimate; in something
that he "loves," according to the profound Scriptural for-
mula, "with all his heart, with all his soul, with all his might"
—and that "something" can never be justified in terms of fact
or reason. Every man, therefore, has his faith, whether he
recognizes it or not, whether he avows it or not; the beliefs
which a man really holds, it is well to remember, are not
necessarily those he affirms with his mouth but those that are
operative in his life.

—WILL HERBERG

Emotion is a fluid that connects all the provinces of our
being; and though we name one of them painting, another
poetry, another religion, they are all interactive . . .

—JOHN JAY CHAPMAN

When power leads man toward arrogance, poetry reminds
him of his limitations. When power narrows the areas of
man's concern, poetry reminds him of the richness and diversity of his existence. When power corrupts, poetry cleanses.

—JOHN F. KENNEDY

I say the profoundest service that poems or any other writings can do for their reader is not merely to satisfy the intellect, or supply something polish'd and interesting, nor even
to depict great passions, or persons or events, but to fill him
with vigorous and clean manliness, religiousness, and give him
good heart as a radical possession and habit. . . . Without
yielding an inch the working-man and working-woman were
to be in my pages from first to last.

—WALT WHITMAN

Most of us succumb to the magnetic property of things and
evaluate events by their tangible results. We appreciate things
that are displayed in the realm of Space. The truth, however,
is that the genuinely precious is encountered in the realm of
Time, rather than in Space. Monuments of bronze live by

the grace of the memory of those who gaze at their form, while moments of the soul endure even when banished to the back of the mind. Feelings, thoughts, are our own, while possessions are alien and often treacherous to the self. To be is more essential than to have. Though we deal with things, we live in deeds.

—ABRAHAM JOSHUA HESCHEL

Work is the other component; not work as a compulsive activity in order to escape aloneness, not work as a relationship to nature which is partly one of dominating her, partly one of worship of and enslavement by the very products of man's hands, but work as creation in which man becomes one with nature in the act of creation.

—ERICH FROMM

As for money, neglect it not: but note, that there is no necessity of being rich: for I told you there be as many miseries beyond riches as on this side of them.

—IZAAK WALTON

Humorous persons do not sit like explosives on a fuse. They are safe and easy comrades. But a wit's tongue is as sharp as a donkey driver's stick. I may gallop the faster for its prodding, yet the touch behind is too persuasive for any comfort.

. . . as I think of my acquaintances, it is those who are humorous in its best and truest meaning rather than those who are witty who give the more profitable companionship.

—CHARLES S. BROOKS

The merit of the following [experiences] are: at a wedding, to cause merriment: among mourners, to keep silent: at a lecture, to listen: at a session, to arrive early: at teaching, to concentrate: in time of fasting, to give charity.

—TALMUD

. . .

Blest, who can unconcernedly find
Hours, days, and years, slide soft away
In health of body, peace of mind
      Quiet by day.
Sound sleep by night; study and ease
Together mix'd, sweet recreation,
And innocence, which most does please
      With meditation.

. . .

—ALEXANDER POPE

Without fullness of experience, length of days is nothing.
When fullness of life has been achieved, shortness of days is
nothing. . . . This experience of fulfillment through wholeness is the true answer to the brevity of man's days.

—LEWIS MUMFORD

Through zealous labor in the performance of a good deed,
we can acquire joy.

God dislikes melancholy and depressed spirits.

Joy is a cure of illness caused by melancholy.

It is the duty of the joyful person to bring to those in sadness
and melancholy a portion of his mood.

—HASIDIC

Man and God...

God does not die on the day when we cease to believe in a
personal diety, but we die on the day when our lives cease to
be illumined by the steady radiance, renewed daily, of a
wonder, the source of which is beyond all reason.

—DAG HAMMARSKJÖLD

Mindfulness of God rises slowly, a thought at a time. Suddenly, we are there. Or is He here, at the margin of our
soul? . . .

*To pray is to take notice of the wonder, to regain a sense of
the mystery that animates all beings, the Divine margin
in all attainments.* Prayer is *our* humble *answer* to the inconceivable surprise of living. It is all we can offer for the
mystery by which we live.

—ABRAHAM JOSHUA HESCHEL

If we could solve all the mysteries of the Universe, we would
be co-equal with God. Every drop of ocean shares its glory
but is not the ocean.

—MAHATMA GANDHI

Fractions: The universe, I am prepared to believe, is governed
by strict laws about which all of us are in doubt. It is always
reassuring, therefore, to see any part of the universal opera-
tion emerge into certainty. What does it matter if our cer-

tainties are infinitesimal as measured against the all? Any
certainty permits the hope that another may lie beyond it,
and another beyond that. It puts us in process toward hope
again. One glimple of law at work sets the conceptual pattern
for all law. And though the sum of truth will not be said at
once, nor perhaps ever, we are all restored to faith in the
act of catching any flaking fraction of it.

—JOHN CIARDI

I am committed more completely than ever before to the
Deposit of Faith, but I am no longer content to say, "God
is thus. Man is thus," and then make an end of it. Whenever
I turn on this high pinnacle, I am confronted with mystery.
I believe in the Godly harmony which is the result of the
eternal creative act. . . . But I do not always hear the harmony. I must wrestle with the cacophony and apparent dis-
cord of the score, knowing that I shall not hear the final
grand resolution until the day I die and, hopefully, am united
with God . . .

—MORRIS L. WEST

Why do we say: "Our God and the God of our fathers"?
There are two kinds of people who believe in God. One
believes because he has taken over the faith of his fathers. . . .
The other has arrived at faith through thinking and studying.
The difference between them is this: The advantage of the
first is that, no matter what arguments may be brought
against it, his faith cannot be shaken; his faith is firm because
it was taken over from his fathers. But there is one flaw in
it: he has faith only in response to the command of man,
and he has acquired it without studying and thinking of
himself. The advantage of the second is that, because he
found God through much thinking, he has arrived at a faith
of his own. But here too there is a flaw: it is easy to shake
his faith by refuting it through evidence. But he who unites
both kinds of faith is invincible. And so we say, "Our God"
with reference to our studies, and "God of our fathers" with
an eye to tradition.

—HASIDIC

A preacher driving along a back road sees one of his parishioners wearily cleaning up a poor, stony field.

"That's a fine job you and the Lord have done cleaning up that rocky field," he shouted.

"Thank you, parson," the man replied. "I wish you could have seen it when the Lord had it all to himself."

—ADLAI E. STEVENSON

He is the Lord of wonders;
His goodness is for all time;
Daily He renews the work of creation.

—WEEKDAY PRAYER BOOK

Yet Thou hast made him but little lower than the angels,
And hast crowned him with glory and honor.
Thou hast made him to have dominion over the works of
    Thy hands;
Thou hast put all things under his feet.

—PSALMS 8:6–7

Freedom consists not in refusing to recognize anything above us, but in respecting something which is above us; for by respecting it, we raise ourselves to it, and, by our very acknowledgment, prove that we bear within ourselves what is higher, and are worthy to be on a level with it.

—JOHANN WOLFGANG VON GOETHE

"And thou shalt love the Lord thy God with all thy heart . . . soul . . . might." (Deuteronomy 6:5) Rabbi Eliezer said: After we are told to love God with our whole life, why are we then told to love Him with all our might, that is, our wealth? There are persons to whom life is more precious than wealth. They are admonished to love Him with all their life. But there are others whose actions indicate that wealth is dearer to them than life. Such people are bidden to love God with all their wealth.

—TALMUD

We praise Thee, O God, for Thy Glory displayed in all the
 creatures of the earth,
In the snow, in the rain, in the wind, in the storm; in all of
 Thy creatures, both the hunters and the hunted.
For all things exist only as seen by Thee, only as known by
 Thee, all things exist
Only in Thy light, and Thy glory is declared even in that
 which denies Thee; the darkness declares the glory of
 light.
Those who deny Thee could not deny, if Thou didst not
 exist; and their denial is never complete, for if it were
 so, they would not exist.
They affirm Thee in living; all things affirm Thee in
 living; the bird in the air, both the hawk and the finch;
 the beast on the earth, both the wolf and the lamb; the
 worm in the soil and the worm in the belly.
Therefore man, whom Thou hast made to be conscious of
 Thee, must consciously praise Thee, in thought and in
 word and in deed.

—T. S. ELIOT

The Elders in Rome were asked: "If God has no pleasure in
an idol, why does He not make an end of it?" To which they
replied: "If men worshiped a thing of which the world had
no need, He would make an end of it: but lo, they worship
the sun and the moon and the stars and the planets: shall God
destroy the world because of fools?"

—MISHNAH

We and God have business with each other; and in opening
ourselves to His influence our deepest destiny is fulfilled.

—WILLIAM JAMES

We do not fret directly against the Lord, but we fret against
religion. "Religion is a failure, else this terrible catastrophe
would never have occurred." This is the statement made on
all sides. But is it religion that is a failure? Have we been
living in a really religious age when this calamity over-

whelmed us? Has there been any doctrine which has remained unassailed during the last two generations; any portion of the Scriptures, which has escaped heartless dissection; any religious symbol or ceremony which was not slighted more or less? Almost every ideal sanctioned by tradition and the consent of humanity has been boldly challenged, whilst many a noble sentiment almost inherent in the race and taken for granted by humanity at large, has been ridiculed and looked upon as an impediment to the perfection of a misunderstood manhood. Everybody at all familiar with the trend of thought could feel that we're standing on a veritable volcano created by the upheavals of the newest methods of 'searching research' which respects as little the new formulae, such as the categoric imperative and conscience, as it does creeds and dogmas.

—SOLOMON SCHECHTER

Religion is, first and foremost, a system of ideas by means of which individuals can envisage the society of which they are members, and the relations, obscure yet intimate, which they bear to it. That is the primordial task of a faith. And though it be metaphorical and symbolical, it is not therefore untrue. On the contrary, it conveys all that is essential in the relations it claims to portray. . . .

—ÉMILE DURKHEIM

The law of the Lord is perfect, restoring the soul;
The testimony of the Lord is sure, making wise the simple.
The precepts of the Lord are right, rejoicing the heart;
The commandment of the Lord is pure, enlightening the eyes.
The fear of the Lord is clean, enduring for ever;
The ordinances of the Lord are true, they are righteous altogether;
More to be desired are they than gold, yea, than much fine gold;
Sweeter also than honey and the honeycomb.
Moreover by them is Thy servant warned;
In keeping of them there is great reward.
Who can discern errors?

Clear Thou me from hidden faults.
Keep back Thy servant also from presumptuous sins,
That they may not have dominion over me; then shall I be
    faultless,
And I shall be clear from great transgression.
Let the words of my mouth and the meditation of my heart
    be acceptable before Thee,
O Lord, my Rock and my Redeemer.

                          —PSALMS 19:8–15

These involve us...

Helping an individual...

A single man [Adam] was created to teach that if one caused
a person to perish it is as though one caused a whole world
to perish.

And he who saves a single person, it is as though he saved the
whole world.

—MISHNAH

"Are you not lonely out here?" asked a visitor of a lighthouse
keeper on an isolated reef. "Not since I saved my first man,"
came the swift answer.

—HARRY EMERSON FOSDICK

I know this well, that if one thousand, if one hundred, if ten
men whom I could name—if ten *honest* men only—aye, if *one*
honest man, if this State of Massachusetts, *ceasing to hold
slaves*, were actually to withdraw from this co-partnership,
and be locked up in the county jail therefor, it would be the
abolition of slavery in America. For it matters not how small
the beginning may seem to be: what is once well done is done
forever.

—HENRY DAVID THOREAU

A man's mind should always be harmoniously attuned to that
of his fellow-man.

—TALMUD

Is not this the fast that I have chosen?
To loose the fetters of wickedness,
To undo the bands of the yoke,
And to let the oppressed go free,
And that ye break every yoke?
Is it not to deal thy bread to the hungry,
And that thou bring the poor that are cast out to thy house?
When thou seest the naked, that thou cover him,
And that thou hide not thyself from thine own flesh?
Then shall thy light break forth as the morning,
And thy healing shall spring forth speedily;
And thy righteousness shall go before thee,
The glory of the Lord shall be thy rearward.

—ISAIAH 58:6–8

There are those who suffer very greatly and cannot tell what
is in their hearts, and they go their ways full of suffering.
But if they meet someone whose face is bright with laughter,
he can quicken them with his gladness. And it is no small
thing to quicken a human being!

—HASIDIC

If we could internationally display on this front some of the
imagination and initiative, determination and sacrifice, that
we show in respect of defence planning and development the
outlook would be more hopeful than it is. The grim fact,
however, is that we prepare for war like precocious giants
and for peace like retarded pygmies.

—LESTER B. PEARSON

"Ye shall walk after the Lord our God." (Deuteronomy 13:5)
But how can a man walk after God who is a devouring fire?
(Deuteronomy 4:24)
It means walk after His attributes, clothe the naked, visit
the sick, comfort the mourner, bury the dead.

—TALMUD

If you want to raise a man from mud and filth, do not think
it is enough to stay on top and reach a helping hand down to
him. You must go all the way down yourself, down into
mud and filth. Then take hold of him with strong hands and
pull him and yourself out into the light.

—HASIDIC

By this time I suppose you have considered the technique of
letting-the-other fellow-do-you a-favor. I am much impressed
by its usefulness as a means of breaking the ice. . . .

—H. A. OVERSTREET

When you deal with them [those who love God], they
seem to you the brothers of modesty; when you talk with
them, they appear to you as sages; when you question them,
as scholars; when you sin against them, as the meek.

—BAHYA IBN PAKUDA

We must broaden the frontiers of our loyalties, never forgetting as we do so that it is the human individual, and not the
state or any other community, in whom ultimate sovereignty
is vested.

—J. WILLIAM FULBRIGHT

. . . A teacher must understand, if he is a teacher, that his
students potentially know everything, no matter how young
they are. You know, a student who is only seventeen has
lived, after all, on earth seventeen years, and that's a good
deal of time. He's been born and he's had parents, he's lived
in houses, he's had friends, he's had sweethearts, he's been
angry, he's been jealous, he's been proud, he's been ambitious,
he's been ashamed. There isn't any passion that he hasn't
experienced in one sense or another. . . .

—MARK VAN DOREN

When Akabia, son of Mahalalel, was dying, his son said to
    him:

"Father, commend me to some of your comrades."

Akabia said to him:

"I will not commend you."

His son said to him: "Is it because of some fault you have
    found in me?"

He said to him:

"No. But your deeds will endear you, and your deeds will
    estrange you."

—MISHNAH

Helping a community ...

Rabbi Judah the Prince asked Rabbi Dosa and Rabbi Ammi to go forth and inspect the cities in the land of Israel.

They came to a city and said to the people: "Have the keepers of the city brought before us."

They brought the overseer and the senator.

Then they said to them: "Are these the keepers of the city? Why, these are the destroyers of the city!"

Then the people asked them: "Who are the keepers of the city?"

Thereupon they answered: "The teachers of the Scriptures and of the Tradition, who keep watch by day and by night, in accordance with the words: 'This book of the law shall not depart out of thy mouth, but thou shalt meditate therein day and night.' " (Joshua 1:8)

—MIDRASH

The Messiah . . . is that which makes man more human, which takes the element of pride out of generosity, which stretches his soul towards others.

—ELIE WIESEL

Religion, it seems to me, functions in an ivory tower—in a quiet and respectable vacuum—when it ceases to inform and inspire, when it misses its social opportunity, when it fails to have impact on people and state. As you well know, the prophets were in the thick of it; their voices rose above the people, and they were eagerly heeded. And what was their message if not chiefly an ethical interpretation of the law?

—ARTHUR J. GOLDBERG

Two things are the purpose of the entire Law: the welfare of the soul and the welfare of the body. The welfare of the soul is achieved through communicating to the mass of the people correct beliefs within their intellectual grasp. Some of these have to be imparted by explicit statements, others by parables, since on the whole the nature of the multitude is not so as to allow them to grasp those things as they are. The welfare of the body is achieved by setting aright the way they live together. This purpose is attained by two things. One of them is to remove injustice from their midst. This means that no man is permitted to do what he wants and has power to do, but is constrained to do only such things as are for the common benefit. The second means is to train every individual in socially useful habits so that the affairs of the state run smoothly.

—MAIMONIDES

Those little Lilliputians, they had big ideas! . . .

In choosing persons for all employments they have more regard to good morals than to great abilities; for, since government is necessary to mankind, they believe that the common size of human understanding is fitted to some station or other, and that Providence never intended to make the management of public affairs a mystery, to be comprehended only by a few persons of sublime genius, of which there seldom are three born in an age: but they suppose truth, justice, temperance, and the like, to be in every man's power; the practice of which virtues, assisted by experience and a good intention, would qualify any man for the service of his country . . .

—JONATHAN SWIFT

Simeon from the village of Sichnin, who was a well-digger, once said to Rabbi Yohanan, son of Zakkai.

"I am as great a man as you!"

"How so?" asked the Rabbi.

"Because when you tell a man or woman to use water which is ceremonially purifying, it is I who provide it for them."

—MIDRASH

> Society is a necessary condition of life in this world and a necessary medium of personal self-realization through community; that is why we hold it to be part of the order of creation.
>
> —WILL HERBERG

Beneath our striving and our hustling, beneath our envies and our jealousies, we all need the same things. We all need affection and the regard of others. We all need the warmth of an abiding place. We all need the free use of our constructive capacities. We all need sustainment and a hope for the future. We all need to be in some sense understood. These needs are compatible as between the members of a community, the near community or the great community.

—R. M. MACIVER

> It is well known that man requires friends all his lifetime. Aristotle explains this in the ninth book of his *Nikomachean Ethics*. When man is in good health and prosperous, he enjoys the company of his friends; in time of trouble he is in need of them; in old age, when his body is weak, he is assisted by them.
>
> —MAIMONIDES

. . . maturing adults . . . would want . . . each on his own or in fellowship with others, to undertake some project for human betterment, some way of bringing more of reasonableness into the human scene.

—H. A. OVERSTREET

"Thou madest man as the fish of the sea" (Habakuk 1:14) . . .
as with the fish of the sea, the big swallow the small, so
with men; were it not for the fear of the Government the
big would swallow the small.

—TALMUD

The world is before you and you need not take it or leave
it as it was when you came in.

—JAMES BALDWIN

. . . as life is action and passion, it is required of a man that
he should share the passion and action of his time at peril of
being judged not to have lived.

—OLIVER WENDELL HOLMES

We must not appoint a leader over the community without
first consulting the people.

—TALMUD

The noblest question in the world is, "What good may I do
in it?"

—BENJAMIN FRANKLIN

If you will lift the load I will lift it too; but if you will not
lift it I will not.

—TALMUD

The power of good action...

"When Moses was grown up . . ." (Exodus 2:11) Why is "was grown up" written twice; "and the child grew up"? (Exodus 2:10)

The first time refers to physical growth, the second time refers to greatness, that is, to spiritual growth.

What was his spiritual greatness? That he "went out unto his brethren." (Exodus 2:11)

—MIDRASH

To love God truly, one must first love man. And if anyone tells you that he loved God and does not love his fellow-man, you will know that he is lying.

—HASIDIC

. . . what is courtesy? Courtesy consists in assuming that everyone else is a gentleman, not in wondering whether he is or not, but in just assuming that he is. To be a gentleman is to be nothing, I say, except a man who thinks all other men are gentlemen.

Now, it may seem naïve sometimes to make this assumption, but it's astonishing how many gentlemen you create by making such an assumption, and how many ladies you can create by assuming that all women are ladies. . . .

—MARK VAN DOREN

[33]

Ben Azzai says: Be quick in carrying out a minor commandment as in the case of a major one, and flee from transgression: for one good deed leads to another good deed and
one transgression leads to another transgression: for the reward for a good deed is another good deed and the reward
for a transgression is another transgression.

—ETHICS OF THE FATHERS

By good conduct is meant . . . common honesty in business
life, faithfulness to duty, ambition in business and profession,
filial obligation, the use of talents, and always and everywhere
simple human kindness and love.

—RANDOLPH BOURNE

"Everyone of us is given the gift of life, and what a strange
gift it is. If it is preserved jealously and selfishly it impover-
ishes and saddens, but if it is spent for others it enriches
and beautifies."

—IGNAZIO SILONE

When a man is singing and cannot lift his voice, and another
comes and sings with him, another who can lift his voice,
the first will be able to lift his voice too. That is the secret
of the bond between the spirits.

—HASIDIC

Forge thy tongue on an anvil of truth
And what flies up, though it be but a spark,
Shall have weight.

—PINDAR

Most arts require long study and application; but the most
useful art of all, that of pleasing, requires only the desire.

—LORD CHESTERFIELD

The art and science of life are even more exacting in their demands than any others. The penetration of moral decisiveness into every aspect of life, and indeed the very conception of life as a science and an art, involves sacrifice of the immediate and tangible for the future and the intangible.

—LOUIS FINKELSTEIN

"Woe to those who are attached to iniquity with weak strands and to sin with a cart rope." (Isaiah 5:18) That is, the beginning of sin is like a thread of a spider's web; its end is like a cart rope.

Rabbi said: He who fulfills one command for his own sake should not rejoice because of that one commandment, but because this one commandment will lead to the fulfillment of many commandments; so too he who commits one sin should not grieve over that one sin: but rather that it leads to many sins. For a good deed creates the way to another good deed and sin incites to sin.

—MIDRASH

But the cause of this error is that this foolish man and his unreasonable companions in the throng regard the whole universe only from the angle of individual existence. Thus every fool thinks that life is there for his sake alone, and as though nothing existed but he. And so, when anything happens that opposes his wishes, he concludes that the whole universe is evil. But if a man would regard the whole universe itself and realize what an infinitesimal part he plays in it, the truth would be clear and apparent to him.

—MAIMONIDES

These continue us...

Providing for others ...

Our Rabbis taught:
When Rabbi Eliezer fell ill, his pupils came to visit him.
They said to him:
"Master, teach us the ways of life, so that by following them,
we may become worthy of life in the coming world."
Then he said to them:
"Watch over the honor of your friends; keep your children
from speculation, and have them sit at the feet of scholars;
and when you pray know before whom you stand. Thus will
you grow worthy of life in the future world."

—TALMUD

The questions which one asks oneself begin, at last, to
illuminate the world, and become one's key to the experience of others. One can only face in others what one can
face in oneself. On this confrontation depends the measure of
our wisdom and compassion.

—JAMES BALDWIN

He who rejoices on the festivals but does not give to the
Holy One, blessed be He, His due share, is selfish. . . . To
give the portion of the Holy One, blessed be He, means to
make glad the poor, according to one's ability.

—ZOHAR

If I were a godfather wishing a gift on a child, it would be that he should always be more interested in other people than himself. That's a *real* gift.

—SIR COMPTON MACKENZIE

"Let the honor of your fellow be as dear to you as your own." (Ethics of the Fathers 2:15) This teaches that even as one looks out for his own honor, so should he look out for his fellow's honor. And even as no man wishes that his own honor be held in ill repute, so should he wish that the honor of his fellow shall not be held in ill repute.

—FATHERS ACCORDING TO RABBI NATHAN

The comfort of having a friend may be taken away, but not that of having had one.

—SENECA

Do not weep, my children. I am not going very far, and I shall see you from there; you will only have to look up at night and you will see me smile. . . . Thus God apportions things. . . . He sees us all, and He knows what He does amid His great stars. . . . Love each other well and always. There is no other thing in the world but that; love one another. . . . My children, I can no longer see clearly. I had other things to say to you, but no matter. Think of me sometimes. . . . I don't know what ails me! I see light. Come nearer yet. I die happy. Let me lay my hands on your beloved heads.

—VICTOR HUGO

Our masters, blessed be their memory, said that the world endures only for the sake of the breath out of the mouths of children who go to school. (From this you see that great is the reward of those who teach children.)

—TALMUD

The ultimate responsibility for good or evil rests with the individual. The things that animate and disturb him are transferable to the group and to government. Public opinion is the accumulation and expression of individual concerns. . . . The educator who prides himself on the advanced learning he imparts to students is actually a purveyor of gross illiteracy if he transmits no awareness of the danger of world anarchy or the means by which it can be eliminated. The scientist who stands tall in his profession is actually a pygmy if he takes no responsibility for what he makes. The titan of industry who presides over efficient and high production is no more than a transient spectator to the demolition of his industry if he fails to comprehend the implications of a world without law.

—NORMAN COUSINS

A rabbi was asked why one does not recite a blessing when giving charity, as we do in performing other commandments.

"Were a blessing required before giving charity, one could give an excuse for not giving at a particular time, that he is not clean enough to pronounce the blessing. Hence we are freed from reciting the blessing so that the needy should be helped without delay."

—HASIDIC

My days among the Dead are past;
    Around me I behold,
Where'er these casual eyes are cast,
    The mighty minds of old:
My never-failing friends are they,
With whom I converse day by day.

.   .   .

    Partake their hopes and fears,
And from their lessons seek and find
Instruction with an humble mind.

My hopes are with the Dead; anon
    My place with them will be,
And I with them shall travel on
    Through all Futurity;
Yet leaving here a name, I trust,
That will not perish in the dust.
              —ROBERT SOUTHEY

"Blessed is he that does righteousness at all times." (Psalms 106:3) This refers to one who nourishes his children well while they are young.

Rabbi Samuel, the son of Nahmani, declared that it refers to one who brings up orphans in his house until he arranges for their marriage.

              —TALMUD

On the Saturday after my birthday I sat down and wrote eight thank you notes. A week later I found them where I put them until my trip to the post office. For a week I had gone my way, confident that eight friends had heard from me, that they were now fully aware of how pleased I was over their gifts. I had felt it—the closeness of communication between us, their warmth and mine—as surely as if the letters had gotten there. The absurdity of my feeling is obvious. Yet a great many people commit similar absurdities every day, assuming that someone *knows* how we feel or appreciate or think or love though nothing has been said to express our feeling or thought or appreciation or love. We're all guilty: husbands to wives, parents to children, children to parents, employee to boss as well as boss to employee.

You don't have to slather on the flattery. The greatest compliments can be paid in three or four words: "I'm proud of you." "Please come." "You're beautiful." "How kind you are." "I need you." "It's more fun if you're here."

              —MARGUERITE JOHNSTON

"And thou shalt love thy neighbor as thyself," (Leviticus 19:18) and the Sages have laid it down as a principle: "What is hateful to you, do not do to your fellow." (Shabbath 31a)

—AKNIN

Raba said . . . "From where do we learn the teaching of our Rabbis that if a person seeks mercy for his fellow, while he himself is in need of the same thing, he will be answered first?" He answered: "It is written: 'And the Lord changed the fortune of Job when he prayed for his friends.' " (Job 42:10)

—TALMUD

Acts of righteousness
and love ...

When Rabbi Pinhas and his disciples discussed wicked or hostile persons, they recalled the advice the Baal Shem Tov once gave to the father of a renegade son: that he should love him more. "When you see," they said, "that someone hates you and does you harm, rally your spirit and love him more than before. That is the only way you can make him turn . . ."

—HASIDIC

. . . knowledge will brighten the sunshine; right is more beautiful than private affection; and love is compatible with universal wisdom.

—RALPH WALDO EMERSON

If you see love as a compromise, a defeat, you're mistaken. It's a victory. Above all in time of war, when men are filled with death. This is the time to love. This is the time to choose. An act of love may tip the balance.

—ELIE WIESEL

The highest wisdom is kindness.

—TALMUD

If you want a world, you will not have justice; if it is justice
you want, there will be no world. You are taking hold of the
rope by both ends—you desire both a world *and* justice—but
if you don't concede a little, the world cannot stand.

—MIDRASH

For social and personal integration we must develop the small
life-promoting occasions for love as well as the grand ones.
Not a day, then, without nurturing or furthering life; without
repairing some deficiency of love in our homes, our villages,
our cities; without caring for a child, visiting the sick, tending
a garden.

—LEWIS MUMFORD

I call heaven and earth to witness that whether it be Jew or
gentile, man or woman, free or bondman—only according to
their acts does the Divine spirit rest upon them.

—MIDRASH

I call heaven and earth to witness against you this day, that
I have set before thee life and death, the blessing and the
curse; therefore choose life, that thou mayest live, thou
and thy seed . . .

—DEUTERONOMY 30:19

Nuptial love maketh mankind; friendly love perfecteth it;
but wanton love corrupteth and embaseth it.

—FRANCIS BACON

We should try to develop concern. We should lead students
not out of the world but into it and with their eyes open.

—ARTHUR G. COONS

. . . the many bad experiences with men have nourished the
meadow of my life as the noblest book could not do, and the
good experiences have made the earth into a garden for me.
. . . I revere books—those that I really read—too much to
be able to love them. But in the most venerable of living

men I always find more to love than to revere: I find in him
something of this world, that is simply there as the spirit
never can be there . . . I knew nothing of books when I came
forth from the womb of my mother, and I shall die without
books, with another human hand in my own.

—MARTIN BUBER

At the time of man's departure from this world, there are
three who plead for him: his family, his money, and his good
deeds.

The first two are not deemed to be valid credentials of personal worth, but a man's good deeds precede him and prepare
him for the road to eternity.

—MIDRASH

Lord, who shall sojourn in Thy tabernacle?
Who shall dwell upon Thy holy mountain?
He that walketh uprightly, and worketh righteousness,
And speaketh truth in his heart;
That hath no slander upon his tongue,
Nor doeth evil to his fellow,
Nor taketh up a reproach against his neighbor;
In whose eyes a vile person is despised,
But he honoreth them that fear the Lord;
He that sweareth to his own hurt, and changeth not;
He that putteth not out his money on interest,
Nor taketh a bribe against the innocent.
He that doeth these things shall never be moved.

—PSALMS 15:1—5

Moral courage and character go hand in hand. . . . a man of
real character is consistently courageous, being imbued with
a basic integrity and a firm sense of principle.

—MARTHA BOAZ

Behold, unto the Lord thy God belongeth the heaven, and the heaven of heavens, the earth, with all that therein is.

He doth execute justice for the fatherless and widow, and loveth the stranger, in giving him food and raiment. Love ye therefore the stranger; for ye were strangers in the land of Egypt.

—DEUTERONOMY 10:14, 18–19

To be rich, to be famous? What do these profit a year hence, when other names sound louder than yours, when you lie hidden away under ground, along with the idle titles engraven on your coffin? But only true love lives after you— follows your memory with secret blessings—or precedes you, and intercedes for you. *Non omnis moriar—*if dying. I yet live in a tender heart or two; nor am lost and hopeless living, if a sainted departed soul loves and prays for me.

—WILLIAM MAKEPEACE THACKERAY

Deeds of kindness are equal in weight to all the commandments.

—TALMUD

"The Lord loves the righteous." (Psalms 146:8)

Says the Holy One, blessed be He: "They love me, and I love them also." And why does the Holy One, blessed be He, love the righteous? Because their righteousness is not a matter of heritage or family.

—MIDRASH

Looking inward ...

Prosperity comes not in anything weighed, measured or counted, but only in things hidden from the eye.

—TALMUD

What shall it profit a man if he gain the whole world and lose his own soul?

—JOHANN WOLFGANG VON GOETHE

The fact that it's difficult to see the signs doesn't necessarily mean that they don't exist. The signs are there to be seen, if we could understand them. . . .

—MARK VAN DOREN

And ye shall seek Me, and find Me, when ye shall search for Me with all your heart.

—JEREMIAH 29:13

A sane and wholesome view of life and death is to be found in the treatment of the text, "[Better is] the day of death than the day of one's birth" (Ecclesiastes 7:1): When a person is born, all rejoice; when he dies, all weep. But it should not be so. On the contrary, when a person is born, there should not be rejoicing because nobody knows what will be his lot and career, whether righteous or wicked, good or bad. When, on the other hand, he dies, it is an occasion for rejoicing if he departed with a good name and left the world peacefully.

This is a parable of two ships making their way through the ocean, one leaving the harbor and the other entering it. People rejoiced over the ship on its departure, but not over the one which was arriving. A clever man stood there and said to them: "My opinion is the opposite of yours. You should not rejoice over the ship which has set out as nobody knows what lies in store for it, what rough seas and storms it may encounter; but when a ship reaches its harbor, all should rejoice that it arrived in safety."

—MIDRASH

The longest journey
Is the journey inwards.
Of him who has chosen his destiny,
Who has started upon his quest
For the source of his being

. . .

—DAG HAMMARSKJÖLD

. . . under inspection the stamp of inwardness is apt to tarnish. We must be silent on our own internal life or it may cease to be internal.

—LOUIS GINZBERG

Of those who, at any given time, profess a religious position, some have been born to it, in the sense that it was communicated to them early in life through the home or church, others achieve it for themselves, and still others have it thrust upon them by social pressures. But though few of them are articulately aware of the logic of their case, most of them sense, even if somewhat inchoately, its fundamental reasonableness, utility, and simplicity.

—MILTON STEINBERG

Pray that your loneliness may spur you into finding something to live for, great enough to die for.

—DAG HAMMARSKJÖLD

Rabbi Sheshet was totally blind. Once, when the entire population of the town went to welcome the king on his visit to the city, Rabbi Sheshet went along with the people.

A scoffing unbeliever said to him: "Whole pitchers go to the well, but why do broken pitchers go there?
Said Rabbi Sheshet, "Come along and you will see that my sight is keener than yours."

The first regiment passed by. As a tumultuous noise was heard, the scoffer shouted: "The king is here!" Said Rabbi Sheshet, "The king is not here yet!" A second regiment passed by, and again there was a loud noise. Again the scoffer exclaimed, "The king is here!" But Rabbi Sheshet said, "The king has not yet arrived." A third regiment appeared and it marched amidst a deep silence. This time Rabbi Sheshet exclaimed, "I am sure that the king is about to appear." And the king did appear.

"How did you know?" asked the scoffer. Rabbi Sheshet then explained to him that earthly majesty, like the heavenly majesty, makes its appearance with the dignity of a still, small voice. (I Kings 19:11 ff)

—TALMUD

What the business man needs most today, it seems to me, is a sense of inner values. He needs to know the purposes of his life. He needs to know the objectives toward which his life is moving. He needs to have his own sense of values by which he can determine his own achievements—because, unless you know what you are trying to do, you can't keep score. At the end you don't know how you have done.

—CLARENCE B. RANDALL

We need . . . to advance from affiliation to affirmation, from external compliance to inner conviction. Solomon Schechter, the great Anglo-American theologian, called our attention to the truism that one cannot love God with his father's heart.

—MAX ARZT

. . . And how do we keep our balance? That I can tell you in a word—tradition!

—JOSEPH STEIN

I do not think seventy years
    is the time of a man or woman,
Nor that seventy millions of years is
    the time of a man or woman,
Nor that years will ever stop
    the existence of me, or
    any one else.

—WALT WHITMAN

Just as the hand, held before the eye, can hide the tallest mountain, so this small earthly life keeps our gaze from the vast radiance and the secrets that fill the world. And he who can draw it from his eyes, as one draws away the hand, will see the great light at the core of the world.

—HASIDIC

Only our spirits can understand beauty, or live and grow with it. It puzzles our minds; we are unable to describe it in words; it is a sensation that our eyes cannot see, derived from both the one who observes and the one who is looked upon. Real beauty is a ray which emanates from the holy of holies of the spirit, and illuminates the body, as life comes from the depths of the earth and gives color and scent to a flower.

—KAHLIL GIBRAN

I believe in the sun even when it is not shining.
I believe in love even when not feeling it. I believe in God even when He is silent.

—INSCRIPTION IN A COLOGNE CELLAR WHERE JEWS HID

It matters not whether you achieve much or little, provided your heart is directed to Heaven.

—TALMUD

2. THE ALIBI "WHAT I DO DOESN'T REALLY MAKE A DIFFERENCE"

Pause a moment.
Look back on your own life.
Haven't you been greatly helped by someone?

Whether by a parent . . .
    whose concern and continuing care shaped your character,

Whether by a teacher . . .
    who was enough of a friend to show you how to continue when you were ready to give up,

Whether by an employer . . .
    whose awareness of your talents opened the way for your success,

Whether by a neighbor . . .
    whose welcome and respect for you and your family made you feel at home where you now live,

Perhaps even by a stranger . . .
    whose unexpected help came just when you needed it.

Remembering such people who made a difference in your life, is it not clear that you also may make a great difference wherever *your* life touches someone else . . .
. . . within your family
. . . where you live
. . . wherever you go.

Why, then, do we so often forget this?

Why do we so frequently feel: *"What I do doesn't really make a difference"?*

We fall into a familiar error, using the wrong yardstick with which to measure goodness.

We think that good actions are really important *only* in times of crisis, only when an extraordinary demand calls for the extraordinary effort.

Yet the time of crisis is but a small part of the opportunity given each of us to contribute to other people's lives.

We need only remember how much and how often—and in how many different ways—our individual act of understanding, of encouragement, of guidance, of personal concern can enlarge the life of someone else, even as enduring good was done for us.

And we need only remember there is no such thing as a *small* good act!

We see this clearly, everywhere around us.

Within the family

Surely, it cannot be the occasional "big gesture" which makes a good parent, or develops a child's character, or creates a joyous family.

Much more, it is the relaxed walk you take with your child . . . listening as well as talking . . . enjoying his companionship as truly as he enjoys yours.

Much more, it is the consistent example set before him of your personal honesty, of your own unselfish acts, of what he sees you accept as right and wrong, and whom you choose to respect.

Much more, it is teaching your child the meaning of the commandment to honor thy father and mother, by the way in which *you* give of yourself to your own parents.

Much more, it is in the way a husband and wife seek each other's counsel, share each other's experience, grasp each day's opportunity to express their mutual need and respect for one another's love.

Of this you can be sure: Nothing can mean more within your family, nothing can replace the intimate gift of your concern and presence.

Where you live

Certainly, to create the kind of neighborhood in which you want to live takes much more than the massive resources and hardest efforts of officials and specialists in housing, education, health and civil rights.

For it is only what *you* do with your neighbors which can make the difference between living with enlarged horizons, in peace—or with fears and suspicions that can only narrow our lives.

It is how *you* welcome a new family, regardless of creed or color, for the individuals they are, because they have every right to the same kind of housing as your own.

It is how *you* urge the same opportunities in schooling for your neighbor's children, whatever their creed or color, that you seek for your own.

It is what *you* do to help a sick or lonely neighbor, in ways no institution can.

It matters not where you live.

In your daily personal actions, you must *be* the kind of neighbor you want to have.

For . . .

Each of us is his neighbor's neighbor.

Wherever you go

We travel more today beyond our own neighborhoods, meeting greater varieties of men and women than any other generation in history.

Yet wherever we go, near or far, we find people whose basic needs and hopes are no different from our closest neighbor.

That is why, as with our neighbors, what we do can make great differences in the life of anyone we meet anywhere.

Surely, we can take the initiative in extending to him the friendship we would like from him.

We can be candid with him, as we want him to be with us.

We can respect and be enriched by his differences, as he can be from ours.

This is but to recognize that he also is made in the image of God.

And that the brotherhood of man is everywhere becoming the neighborhood of men.

In our changing world, there are fundamental realities which do not change.

One of these is the power given each of us to increase goodness in the world through our individual acts.

Our opportunities to do this are always close at hand, every day: within our family, where we live, wherever we go.

That is why we can never use the excuse: *"But what I do doesn't really make a difference."*

For . . .

As our fathers were taught in ancient times, so it remains true for all of us today:

"To save a single life is to save the world." (Mishnah Sanhedrin, 4)

You make a difference within the family...

Husband and wife...

It was the custom [in ancient Judea] to plant a cedar tree when a boy was born, and to plant a pine tree when a girl was born. When they were married, the canopy was made of woven branches from both trees.

—TALMUD

Whoever undertakes a long journey, if he be wise, makes it his business to find out an agreeable companion. How cautious then should he be, who is to take a journey for life, whose fellow-traveler must not part with him but at the grave; his companion at bed and board and everywhere; as the wife must be to the husband! She is no such sort of warp that a man can be rid of when he pleases; no exchange, no sale, no alienation can be made . . .

—MIGUEL DE CERVANTES

Whoso findeth a wife findeth a great good,
And obtaineth favor of the Lord.

—PROVERBS 18:22

I was ever of opinion, that the honest man who married and brought up a large family did more service than he who continued single and only talked of population. From this motive, I had scarcely taken orders a year before I began to think seriously of matrimony, and chose my wife as she did her wedding-gown, not for a fine glossy surface, but such qualities as would wear well. To do her justice, she was a good-natured notable woman; and as for breeding, there were few country ladies who could show more.

—OLIVER GOLDSMITH

Whoever marries a woman for her money will have disreputable children.

—TALMUD

An Emperor said to Rabbi Gamliel: "Your God is a thief because it is written, 'The Lord God caused a deep sleep to fall upon Adam and he slept; and He took one of his ribs.' " (Genesis 2:21)

The Rabbi's daughter said to her father: "Leave him to me: I will answer him."

She then said to the Emperor: "Give me an officer [to investigate a complaint]."

"For what purpose?" he asked.

She replied: "Thieves broke into our house during the night and stole a silver ewer belonging to us, but left a gold one behind."

"Would that such a thief visited me every day," he exclaimed.

"Was it not then a splendid thing for the first man when a single rib was taken from him and a woman to attend him was supplied in its stead?" she retorted.

—TALMUD

The best marriages, like the best lives, were both happy and unhappy. There is even a kind of necessary tension, a certain tautness between the partners that gave the marriage strength, like the tautness of a full sail. You went forward on it.

—ANNE MORROW LINDBERGH

God did not make woman from man's head, that she should
not rule over him; nor from his feet, that she should not be
his slave, but from his side, that she should be near his heart.

—MIDRASH

Rabbi Helbo taught: A husband should treat his wife honor-
ably for she is the real source of blessing in a household.

—TALMUD

Marriage has many pains, but celibacy has no pleasures.

—SAMUEL JOHNSON

. . . that perfect disinterestedness and self-devotion of which
man seems to be incapable, but which is sometimes found in
woman.

—THOMAS BABINGTON MACAULAY

The life I have chosen as wife and mother entrains a whole
caravan of complications. It involves a house in the suburbs
and either household drudgery or household help which
wavers between scarcity and nonexistence for most of us. It
involves food and shelter; meals, planning, marketing, bills,
and making the ends meet in a thousand ways. It involves
not only the butcher, the baker, the candlestickmaker but
countless other experts to keep my modern house with its
modern "simplifications" (electricity, plumbing, refrigerator,
gas-stove, oil burner, dish-washer, radios, car, and numerous
other labor-saving devices) functioning properly. It involves
health; doctors, dentists, appointments, medicine, cod-liver
oil, vitamins, trips to the drugstore. It involves education,
spiritual, intellectual, physical; schools, school conferences,
car-pools, extra trips for basket-ball or orchestra practice;
tutoring; camps, camp equipment and transportation. It involves clothes, shopping, laundry, cleaning, mending, letting
skirts down and sewing buttons on, or finding someone else
to do it. It involves friends, my husband's, my children's, my
own, and endless arrangements to get together; letters, invi-
tations, telephone calls and transportation hither and yon.

—ANNE MORROW LINDBERGH

A woman of valor who can find?
For her price is far above rubies.
                                    —PROVERBS 31:10

. . . we loved each other tenderly, and our fondness increased
as we grew old. There was, in fact, nothing that could make
us angry with the world or with each other. We had an
elegant house, situated in a fine country, and a good neighborhood. The year was spent in moral or rural amusements, in
visiting our rich neighbors and relieving such as were poor.
                                    —OLIVER GOLDSMITH

[Rabbi Judah ibn Tibbon bequeathed this "will" to his son
Samuel]: "I command you to honor your wife to your ut-
most capacity . . . treat her with consideration and respect.
To act otherwise is the way of the contemptible."
                                    —HEBREW ETHICAL WILLS

                         . . . The widest land
Doom takes to part us, leaves thy heart in mine
With pulses that beat double. What I do
And what I dream include thee, as the wine
Must taste of its own grapes . . .
                —ELIZABETH BARRETT BROWNING

A Roman lady asked Rabbi Yosi, the son of Rabbi Halafta:
"In how many days did the Holy One, blessed be He, create
the Universe?" "In six days," he answered. "What has He
been doing since then, up to the present?" "He has been ar-
ranging marriages." "Is that his occupation? I, too, could do
it. I possess many male and female slaves, and in a very short
while I can match them up." He said to her: "If it is a simple
thing in your eyes, it is as difficult to the Holy One, blessed
be He, as dividing the Red Sea."

They then parted. What did she do? She summoned a
thousand male slaves, set them in rows, and arranged marriages for them all. The next day they appeared before her,

one with a cracked forehead, another with a patched eye, and another with a broken leg. She asked them: "What is the matter with you?" One female said: "I don't want him." Another male said: "I don't want her." She forthwith sent for the Rabbi and said to him: "There is no god like your God and your Torah is true. What you told me is quite correct." "Didn't I tell you," said the Rabbi, "matchmaking is as difficult to the Holy One as dividing the Red Sea."

—MIDRASH

Parents and children...

A father complained to the Baal Shem that his son had fore-
saken God. "What, Rabbi, shall I do?"

"Love him more than ever," was the Baal Shem's reply.

—HASIDIC

He that spareth his rod hateth his son;
But he that loveth him chasteneth him betimes.

—PROVERBS 13:24

I suggest that to put the problem of growing up in terms of
"discipline," whether in one extreme form or another, is a
barren way of putting it. Every child needs and wants a sense
of limits—a framework of continuity which furnishes the
boundaries for his life, and prevents him from feeling rudder-
less. But every child also needs the sense of being wanted—
that is to say, the feeling of being part of rich functional
relationships with his family and with his fellows outside the
family.

Some parents make the mistake of thinking that to give a
child his complete freedom solves his problems. It doesn't.
But other parents make the opposite mistake of thinking that

they can "train up the child in the way he should go," and that a stern discipline solves his problems. It doesn't. You can't substitute either rigid codes or an unlimited checking-account in place of warm and living personal relationships that operate within a frame of limits.

—MAX LERNER

Correct thy son, and he will give thee rest; Yea, he will give delight unto thy soul.

—PROVERBS 29:17

A man shall not let his yoke rest heavily upon his children, nor shall he be exacting with them concerning the honor due to him, lest he cause them to stumble. He shall forgive them . . .

—JOSEPH KARO

And these words, which I command thee this day, shall be upon thy heart; and thou shalt teach them diligently unto thy children, and shalt talk of them when thou sittest in thy house, and when thou walkest by the way, and when thou liest down, and when thou risest up.

—DEUTERONOMY 6:6–7

Your son at five is your master, at ten your slave, at fifteen your double, and after that your friend or foe, depending on his bringing up.

—ORIENTAL TALE

The appeal to wants, then, presupposes, first of all, an understanding of the fine, worthwhile wants that *can* be aroused in children; and secondly, an intelligence capable of opening up opportunities and devising situations which will arouse those wants. The parent, in short, is to be, in the main, not a giver-of-commands but an opener-up-of-opportunities . . .

No appeal to a reason that is not also an appeal to a want is ever effective.

H. A. OVERSTREET

Rabbi Zera ruled: One should not promise a child something
and then not give it to him, because he will learn lying.

—TALMUD

As I grew up, I learned that there are all sorts of people in
the world, and that selfishness and greed and envy are, to
say the least, very common in the human heart; but I never
could be thankful enough that my father was honest and
simple, and that his love of truth and justice had grown
into his being as naturally as the oaks were rooted to the earth
along the little stream.

I know that my mother was an energetic, hard-working,
and in every way strong woman, although I did not know
it or think about it then. I know it now, for as I look back
to my childhood and see the large family that she cared for,
almost without help, I cannot understand how she did it all,
especially as she managed to keep well informed on the topics
of the day, and found more time for reading and study than
any of her neighbors did.

It must be that any intelligent parent who really understands
life would be able to make his children feel a companionship
greater than any other they could know.

—CLARENCE DARROW

A man should never threaten his child, but punish him at
once, or say nothing.

—TALMUD

Love thy children with impartial love; the hope oft errs that
you place on the more promising, and all your joy may come
from him that you have kept in the background.

—BENEDICT OF OXFORD

"Thus shalt thou say to the house of Jacob, and tell the children of Israel." That hour when the Torah was given to us,
Moses, our master, peace be with him, was bidden to speak
first to the house of Jacob, and this means to the women.

And why was he bidden to speak first to the women? Because
it is they who send their sons to school; because they keep an
eye upon their sons, so that these may occupy themselves

with the Torah; because they tend them when they come home from school, and move their hearts with good words, so that their longing be directed to the Torah, and they watch over them, lest they go idle instead of learning the Torah; because they teach them the fear of sin, even in childhood, as it is written: "Train up a child in the way he should go, and even when he is old, he will not depart from it." (Proverbs 22:6)

—RABBI JONAH

The talk of a child in the street is that of his father and mother.

—TALMUD

Be fruitful, not prudent: increase and multiply your children, not the ciphers in your bank account. . . . Life and more life! Life before the means of living! A higher and better life in the home, in order to offset the deprivations and sacrifices that these perilous times will inflict on all of us. Our homes and our communities must, even as physical structures, express the central importance of the family; they must be built on a human scale, and wear a friendly face. They must be designed out of love, not merely out of economy; and they must be designed to make love possible.

—LEWIS MUMFORD

My son! Make your books your companions, let your cases and shelves be your pleasure grounds and gardens. Bask in their paradise, gather their fruit, pluck their roses, take their spices and their myrrh. If your soul be satiate and weary, change from garden to garden, from furrow to furrow, from prospect to prospect. Then will your desire renew itself and your soul be filled with delight!

—JUDAH IBN TIBBON

I am always for getting a boy forward in his learning; for that is a sure good. I would let him at first read any English book which happens to engage his attention; because you have done a great deal when you have brought him to have entertainment from a book. He'll get better books afterwards.

—SAMUEL JOHNSON

Hear, my son, the instruction of thy father,
And forsake not the teaching of thy mother . . .
—PROVERBS 1:8

"Parents shouldn't lie to their children—not even when they think it's for their good. Even a little lie is dangerous; it deteriorates the conscience."
—PABLO CASALS

The mistake a lot of guys make, they're always pushin' their kids. "Don't just sit there," they tell 'em. "Go do something. Go play ball, go watch the TV, go annoy the neighbors." Not me. I see to it my kids have a chance to get bored.
—ROBERT WELLS

My son, give God all honor and the gratitude which is His due. Thou hast need of Him, but He needs thee not. Put no trust in thy mere physical well-being here below. . . . Visit the sick and suffering man, and let thy countenance be cheerful when he sees it, but not so that thou oppress the helpless one with gaiety. . . . Respect the poor man by gifts whose hands he knows not of; be not deaf to his beseechings, deal not hard words out to him. From a wicked neighbor, see that thou keep aloof, and spend not much of thy time among the people who speak ill of their brother-man; be not as the fly that is always seeking sick and wounded places; and tell not of the faults and failings of those about thee.
—ELIEZER BEN ISAAC

Children are often cruel from want of thought.

Ah, my boys, youth is the time to learn: it is too late after the cares of the world fall on our shoulders.
—JOHANN DAVID WYSS

Honor thy father and thy mother, that thy days may be long upon the land which the Lord thy God giveth thee.
—EXODUS 20:12

The home...

Better is a dry morsel, and quietness therewith,
Than a house full of feasting with strife.

—PROVERBS 17:1

Rabbi Yosi said: Never have I called my wife, "my wife"
by that word but always, "my Home."

—TALMUD

No one can approach through winter darkness a house from
whose windows light shines out on the snow without feeling
quieted and heartened. Psychic subtleties may be active in
such a response, but there is no need to invoke them; for the
obvious facts provide all the explanation we require. A house
means warmth and shelter, light means human society.

—BERNARD DE VOTO

Who loves his wife as himself, honors her more than himself, leads his sons and daughters in the right path, and arranges for their marriage, to him the text refers, "you shall
know that your tent is in peace." (Job 5:24)

—TALMUD

A man, however fallen, who loves his home, is not wholly
lost.

—BENJAMIN DISRAELI

A man should spend less than his means on food and drink for himself, up to his means on his clothes, and above his means on honoring his wife and children, because they are dependent upon him, while he is dependent upon Him who spake and the Universe came into being.

—TALMUD

In the Jewish life I knew there was a trinity to whom we appealed or expressed our fears. A small accident would evoke *"Mammenyu"* (beloved Mother), a larger mishap would bring forth *"Tottenyu"* (beloved Father), and a shock would provoke *"Gottenyu"* (beloved God). A disaster could evoke an appeal to all three.

Mother, Father and God represented the core of Jewish family life. Every home depended on the warmth and care given by Mother, the strength and security given by Father, and the omnipresence and omnipotence of God. Mother was there when you were ailing or hungry or cold, Father was always handy to protect you, and God was available for everything.

—DORE SCHARY

Beside our need for a meaning, also a need for human intimacy without conventional trappings—for the experience of a circle where power expresses itself in meaningful and beautiful forms.

—DAG HAMMARSKJÖLD

The role of the home as a school for character has never been more important than today. The most urgent issue before us may be whether civilization can survive displacement of the home in this respect. Where else can the emotions be trained so that one will find happiness in righteousness? And if the emotions are not so trained, can one expect the intellectual conviction of what is right to win the struggle against emotional bias toward what is self-centered?

—LOUIS FINKELSTEIN

"My shtetl" is the people who live in it, not the place or the buildings or the street. "My home" is the family and the family activities, not the walls or the yard or the broken-down fence.

—MARK ZBOROWSKI AND ELIZABETH HERZOG

Immorality in the home is like a worm on vegetables.

—TALMUD

Moral and religious education consist in training the feelings and daily habits. . . . It is the home, the family, which gives us the moral or religious education we really receive . . .

—JOHN STUART MILL

Where could there be a more favorable background for sympathetic instruction and effortless learning than a really harmonious family home? For security is in such a home and the awareness of being loved, guidance on the one hand and the relaxation that comes from confidence on the other. In a world full of doubts and disapprovals, here may be faith, unreserved acceptance, and fond admiration to blandish away that carking distrust of oneself.

—EDMOND CAHN

. . . the family is the primary area where feelings can be fully expressed; and the emotional, tender, passionate sides of life have become concentrated within our small family circles. Increasingly, the heart is where the home is.

—KENNETH KENISTON

A man asked the Kotzker advice regarding the wisdom of moving from his native town in order to improve his circumstances. The Rabbi told the following story:

"A certain Jew of Cracow dreamed several times that there was a treasure near a mill awaiting his arrival to dig it up. He left his house early in the morning and dug carefully, but did not find the money. The miller asked the reason for digging near his mill, and when the explanation had been given he exclaimed: 'Why, I dreamed that there is a treasure in the courtyard of a certain man in Cracow,' and he named the digger himself. The man promptly returned to his home, and uncovered the treasure in his own yard."

"You see now," added the Rabbi. "Sometimes a man can find a treasure in his own home."

—HASIDIC

You make a difference
where you live...

Neighbors...

Question: We are commanded to love our neighbor as ourselves. How can I do this if my neighbor has wronged me?

Answer: You must understand these words rightly. Love
your neighbor as something which you yourself are. For all
souls are one. Each is a spark from the original soul, and this
soul is inherent in all souls, just as your soul is inherent in all
the members of your body. It may come to pass that your
hand will make a mistake and strike you. But would you
then take a stick and chastise your hand because it lacked
understanding, and so increase your pain? It is the same if
your neighbor, who is of one soul with you, wrongs you
because of his lack of understanding. If you punish him,
you only hurt yourself.

—HASIDIC

You hold a block of metal in your hand. And it's solid. And
yet within the metal, there are molecules. All moving by
laws of their own. Press a block of pure gold against a block
of steel, one against the other—then when you separate them,
they seem unchanged. But not really. A good physical chem-
ist will show you that when they've been in contact, invisible
flecks of gold molecules have wandered across the barrier
of structure, and buried themselves in the molecular structure

of the steel. And the molecules of steel, somehow, into the structure of the gold . . .

I think . . . that when people are pressed close, they act the same way. Part of you enters them, part of them enters you. . . . Long after you forget the names and faces . . . they're still part of you . . . sometimes it's frightening to think . . . that every person you've ever hated, or feared, or ran away from is part of you.

. . . I think it means you carry inside you every person you've ever learned from, every friend you ever knew.

—THEODORE H. WHITE

A companion can be gained only with the greatest difficulty. Hence they say: "Let a man gain a companion for himself, one who will read with him, learn with him, eat and drink with him, and share his secrets—'for two are better than one.' " (Ecclesiastes 4:9)

—MIDRASH

After the heavenly sacred fact of being a child of God, nothing is as great in human existence as the earthly sacred fact of being a brother of men.

—MARTIN BUBER

. . . people must be taught about the evil effects of prejudice. They must be helped to understand why they have developed prejudices. It means trying to show them that it is unfair and stupid to condemn whole groups, that in every group they will find about the same proportion of people whom they like or dislike; that each man must be judged by himself, on his own merits and faults.

—PRESIDENT'S COMMITTEE ON CIVIL RIGHTS

It is written: "Reprove a wise man and he will love you." (Proverbs 9:8) Rabbi Yosi, the son of Hamma, said: "A love without reproof is no love; a peace where there has been no reproof is no peace."

—MIDRASH

In truly perfect friendship, wherein I presume to have some
skill and well-grounded experience, I gave my selfe more
unto my friend than I draw him unto me. I doe not onely
rather love to do him good, then he should doe any to me,
but also that he should rather doe good unto himselfe then
unto me: For then doth he me most good when he doth it to
himselfe.

—MONTAIGNE

. . . see to it that you love your neighbor in the same manner
in which you love the people of your house, for this love is
graven in your heart. Cherish their honor and their will to the
utmost of your ability, and do their will as though it were
your own. And if your neighbor is guilty of a blameworthy
act, do not hate him for it, for this would only prove that
you did not love him before. For if you loved him, you
would be sorrowful and grieved to hear that he has done
something ugly, just as you would be sad if they told you
the like about your child or your brother. Him you would
rebuke with devotion, with friendly words, and with none
other present—as is proper toward one you love and who
lives at the very core of your heart—and you would ask him
what caused him to act as he did, or the like. According to
the words, "Thou shalt not hate thy brother in thy heart:
thou shalt surely rebuke thy neighbor" (Leviticus 19:17):
that is to say, rebuke him with words spoken alone, face to
face with him. And if you are separated from each other, at
least you must not "bear sin because of him" (Leviticus
19:17), but "in righteousness shalt thou judge thy neighbor"
(Leviticus 19:15), and you must not condemn him until
life has put you in his position. For it is possible that in his
position and with a like cause, you yourself would act much
more reprehensibly than your neighbor. In no case, therefore,
may you hate him, rather shall your great love and mercy
fill you with sorrow and grief concerning the disaster that
has befallen him.

—JACOB BEN WOLF KRANZ

Be courteous to all, but intimate with few; and let those few
be well tried before you give them your confidence. True
friendship is a plant of slow growth, and must undergo and
withstand the shocks of adversity before it is entitled to the
appellation. Let your heart feel for the afflictions and dis-
tresses of everyone, and let your hand give in proportion to
your purse . . .

—GEORGE WASHINGTON

What you must do is love your neighbor as yourself. There
is no one who knows your many faults better than you! But
you love yourself notwithstanding. And so you must love
your neighbor, no matter how many faults you see in him.

—HASIDIC

Friendship is the next Pleasure we may hope for: and
where we find it not at Home, or have no Home to find it in,
we may seek it abroad. It is an Union of Spirits, a Marriage
of Hearts, and the Bond thereto Vertue.

There can be no Friendship where there is no Freedom.
Friendship loves a Free Air, and will not be penned up in
straight and narrow Enclosures. It will speak freely, and act
so too; and take nothing ill where no ill is meant; nay, where
it is, 'twill easily Forgive, and forget too, upon small
Acknowledgments.

—WILLIAM PENN

He who raises the son of his neighbor is accounted as if he
gave birth to him.

—MIDRASH

Friends also follow the laws of divine necessity; they gravi-
tate to each other, and cannot otherwise . . .

—RALPH WALDO EMERSON

To sin against a fellow-man is worse than to sin against the Creator. The man you harmed may have gone to an unknown place, and you may lose the opportunity to beg his forgiveness. The Lord, however, is everywhere and you can always find Him when you seek Him.

—HASIDIC

If you have done your fellow man a little wrong, let it be a great wrong in your eyes and go and rectify it. If you have done him much good, let it be little in your eyes. If he has done you a little good, let it be great in your eyes. If he has done you a great wrong, let it be little in your eyes.

—FATHERS ACCORDING TO RABBI NATHAN

Converting an enemy
into a friend...

Who is mighty? He who turns an enemy into a friend.
—FATHERS ACCORDING TO RABBI NATHAN

Abraham Lincoln was questioned by one of his advisors as follows: "Mr. President, I cannot understand you. You treat your enemies with such kindness. It would seem to me that you should want to destroy them."

"My dear fellow," said the President, "I do destroy my enemy when I make him into a friend."
—ANONYMOUS

To understand is not only to pardon, but in the end to love.
—WALTER LIPPMANN

Rabbi Mihal gave this command to his sons: "Pray for your enemies that all may be well with them. And should you think this is not serving God, rest assured that, more than all our prayers, this love is indeed the service of God."
—HASIDIC

"To forgive oneself"—? No, that doesn't work: we have to *be forgiven*. But we can only believe this is possible if we ourselves can forgive.
—DAG HAMMARSKJÖLD

One of Baal Shem's disciples delighted in the saying that the most hardened sinners were not to be despaired of, but prayed for.

—SOLOMON SCHECHTER

It is written: "Am I a God near at hand . . . and not a God afar off?" (Jeremiah 23:23) "Afar off" refers to the wicked. "Near at hand" refers to the righteous. God says: "Do I want him who is already close to me, do I want the righteous? Why, I also want him who is afar off, I want him who is wicked!"

—HASIDIC

Rabbi Pinhas of Koretz: When someone despises you and does you injury, you shall strengthen yourself and love him more than before. Through such love you bring him to the turning. Therefore one shall also love the evil, only their evil deeds shall one hate.

—HASIDIC

My brothers, seek counsel of another, for therein lies the way out of error and futile repentance. The wisdom of the many is your shield against tyranny. For when we turn to one another for counsel we reduce the number of our enemies.

—KAHLIL GIBRAN

A man goes on his way, and sees a donkey of his fellow fallen beneath his burden; he gives him a hand and helps him unload and reload; then they go into the inn together and the owner of the donkey says: "How he loves me and I thought he hated me!" Then they speak to each other and become reconciled to one another.

What brings it about that they become reconciled to one another? Because the one obeyed the commandment of the Law: "If you see the ass of him that hates you lying under his burden, you shall surely help him." (Exodus 23:5) And so it is written: "Her [wisdom's] ways are ways of pleasantness and all her paths are peace." (Proverbs 3:17)

—MIDRASH

Belong ever to the persecuted, rather than to the persecutors.

—TALMUD

Ben Azzai quoted the verse, "This is the book of the generations of Adam" (Genesis 5:1), and said: "This is the greatest principle of the Law." Rabbi Akiba said: "Thou shalt love thy neighbor as thyself" (Leviticus 19:18) is the greatest principle in the Law."

Do not say: "Because I am despised, so may my neighbor be cursed with me!" "If you act thus," said Rabbi Tanhuma, "know whom you despise, namely a being made in the image of God."

—MIDRASH

I use hate as a weapon to defend myself; had I been strong, I would never have needed that kind of weapon.

—KAHLIL GIBRAN

We should also pray for the wicked among the peoples of the world; we should love them too. As long as we do not pray in this way, as long as we do not love in this way, the Messiah will not come.

—HASIDIC

The Rabbis taught: It says, "You shall not hate your brother in your heart." (Leviticus 19:17) For a man might think: I must not strike him or beat him or curse him, but I may hate him. Therefore it says, "In your heart."

—TALMUD

Giving of oneself...

"Whosoever shall be called by the name of the Lord shall be delivered." (Joel 3:5)

But how is it possible for a man to be called by the name of the Holy One, blessed be He? As the All Present is called compassionate and gracious, so be you also compassionate and gracious and offering free gifts to all . . . "as He is called loving in all His ways" (Psalms 145:17), be you also loving.

—MIDRASH

". . . It is people that count. You put yourself into people; they touch other people; these others still, and so you go on working forever."

—ALICE FREEMAN PALMER

A little farmer boy, having been left an orphan at an early age, was unable to read, but had inherited a large, heavy prayer book from his parents. On the Day of Atonement he brought it into the Synagogue, laid it on the reading desk, and, weeping, cried out: "Lord of Creation! I do not know how to pray; I do not know what to say—I give Thee the entire prayer book."

—HASIDIC

Goodness is something so simple; always to live for others, never to seek one's own advantage.

—DAG HAMMARSKJÖLD

The "new self" that emerges once we achieve deliverance from self-enclosed egocentricity brings a new power for life and introduces a subtle transformation into every aspect of the personality. . . . The self is opened to other selves in genuine community. The entire scale of values by which we live undergoes a radical change; new motives arise and what was once so prone to frustrate and distract now loses its power over us. Organized about its true center, life regains its freedom and wholeness. The victory has been won.

—WILL HERBERG

In the last analysis, what does the word "sacrifice" mean? Or even the word "gift"? He who has nothing can give nothing. The gift is God's—to God.

—DAG HAMMARSKJÖLD

I strive as much in small as I labor in great enterprises . . .

—MONTAIGNE

Love risks degenerating into obsession, friendship is never anything but sharing.

—ELIE WIESEL

Better is he who shows a smiling countenance than he who offers milk to drink.

—TALMUD

When I have attempted to join myself to others by services, it proved an intellectual trick—no more. They eat your service like apples, and leave you out. But love them, and they feel you, and delight in you all the time.

—RALPH WALDO EMERSON

Once a disciple of Rabbi Akiba became ill and no one visited him. Rabbi Akiba, however, entered the sick man's room, arranged that it be swept and cleaned, placed the pillow in order, and the like. All this assisted the recovery of the disciple. He exclaimed: "Oh master, thou hast revived me."

When Rabbi Akiba departed, he said: "Whosoever neglects to visit a friendless sick person is as if one shed his blood."

—TALMUD

"Why me?" he kept mumbling, "with so many good prophets
    to choose from.
Nineveh? Stick out my neck? I could ruin myself, my repu-
    tation.
Suppose, some day, I should run for office—why should I
    rock the boat?
Why couldn't He leave me alone? It was nice the way it was.
    Who'd vote
for a disturber of the peace? And yet . . . someone should
    speak to them;
someone should 'go and speak out against it.' " Taking French
    leave of Him
for Tarshish, end of the map, to sit it out till it would blow
    over,
he learned the perverse serendipity of disowning danger:
the self-entertainment in pursuit of safety. His name almost a
    curse,
tempest-wracked without, within adversity avalanched with
    the storm.
In the black stillness of the depths, "someone," like the
    heckler in the dark,
kept tugging at the coat-tails of his mind. "Someone!"—all
    he could hear,
re-echoed loudly through his lungs, both plea and answer
    to salvation:
to do regardless, inevitably the thing that must be done.

—GERSON SILVERSTEIN

There are friends that one hath to his own hurt;
But there is a friend that sticketh closer than a brother.
—PROVERBS 18:24

Among Orientals giving is a privilege . . .
—ELIE WIESEL

. . . if one gives his fellow all the good gifts in the world
with a downcast face, Scripture accounts it to him as though
he had given him naught. But if he receives his fellow with
a cheerful countenance, even though he gives him naught,
Scripture accounts it to him as though he had given him all
the good gifts in the world.
—FATHERS ACCORDING TO RABBI NATHAN

You make a difference wherever you go...

One world ...

"Shall one man sin, and will You be wroth with all the congregation?" (Numbers 16:22)

Rabbi Simeon, son of Yohai, taught, it is like a company of men on board a ship. One of them took a drill and began to bore a hole under him.

"What are you doing?"

He replied: "What has that to do with you? Am I not making the hole under my seat?"

They answered: "But the water will enter and drown us all."

—MIDRASH

To achieve peace—through justice—will prove a wrenching task. We will have to let go of traditional rhetoric, stereotyped thought, preconceptions, and everything else that inhibits man from fulfilling himself. We wish to cooperate, not compete, so that the family of Man might become one. We see what can be. And we seek the ineffable. We will never grasp it in this life, but we can reach out—and live.

—EDWARD M. KEATING

The belief in a single creation after which the Master withdrew from his completed work, is erroneous and heretical. The vivifying power is never withdrawn from the world which it animates. Creation is continuous; an unending manifestation of the goodness of God. All things are an affluence from the two divine attributes of Power and Love, which express themselves in various images and reflections.

—SOLOMON SCHECHTER

Men frequently think that the evils in the world are more numerous than the good things; many sayings and songs of the nations dwell on this idea. They say that the good is found only exceptionally, while evil things are numerous and lasting. The origin of this error is to be found in the circumstance that men judge of the *whole universe* by examining one single person only. If anything happens to him contrary to his expectation, forthwith he concludes that the whole universe is evil. . . . We seek relief from our own faults; we suffer from evils which we inflict on ourselves, and we ascribe them to God who is far from connected with them. As Solomon explained it: "The foolishness of man perverteth his way, and his heart fretteth against the Lord." (Proverbs 19:3)

—MAIMONIDES

"How beautiful is our earth!" exclaimed Major Gagarin as he came down from space.

"Man, that view is tremendous!" shouted Colonel Glenn, looking at the same view.

These two men have more in common than either has with the ideologists of conquest. This is not just Pollyanna talk. Wars start in the blind, angry hearts of men. But it is hard to hate those who toil and hope and discover beside you in a common human venture. The Glenns of our world could be new men in a quite new sense—the new men, who, having seen our little planet in a wholly new perspective, will be ready to accept as a profound spiritual insight the unity of mankind.

—ADLAI E. STEVENSON

It is true that the whole world will not change if I change.
But the change in myself is the premise of the greater change.

—KARL JASPERS

Twenty thousand years ago the family was the social unit.
The social unit has now become the world, in which may
be fairly said that each person's welfare affects that of every
other. In such a civilization, the importance of good will
among men becomes a matter of unprecedented urgency.

Love of one's neighbor is the natural attitude for those who
recognize that all men may become God's children.

—ARTHUR H. COMPTON

Every death leaves a scar, and every time a child laughs it
starts healing.

—ELIE WIESEL

The major problem on earth is not the bomb. The bomb is
actually the product of the problem. The main problem is
that the human imagination has not yet expanded to the point
where it comprehends its own essential unity. People are not
yet aware of themselves as a single interdependent species
requiring the proper performance of certain vital services
if the human race is to be sustained. They have developed a
world reach without a world consciousness.

—NORMAN COUSINS

At the time when all members of the human body suffer
through an illness, then one member must be operated upon
so that all the remaining members may recover. . . . So it is
with the children of the world; its members are to each other
like members of the human body, each to the other.

—ZOHAR

This is the secret of the Unity of God: no matter where I take hold of a shred of it, I hold the whole of it. And since the teachings and all the commandments are radiations of his being, he who lovingly does one commandment utterly and to the core, and in this one commandment takes hold of a shred of the Unity of God, holds the whole of it in his hand, and has fulfilled all.

—HASIDIC

Endowed with the wonderful endowment of the human mind, we have duties toward all the living beings on earth, with whom we are really one and indivisible.

—CHAKRAVARTI RAJAGOPALACHARI

On a group of theories one can found a school; but on a group of values one can found a culture, a civilization, a new way of living together among men.

—IGNAZIO SILONE

Before the Endlessness of God, the highest saint and the lowliest commoner are equal.

—HASIDIC

A youngster was carrying a boy much heavier and bigger than himself. A passer-by stopped him and asked: "Isn't he too heavy for you?" The youngster answered: "He's not heavy, he's my brother."

—ANONYMOUS

The forlorn Irish Widow applies to her fellow-creatures, as if saying, "Behold I am sinking, bare of help: ye must help me! I am your sister, bone of your bone; one God made us: ye must help me!" They answer, "No, impossible; thou art no sister of ours." But she proves her sisterhood; her typhus-fever kills *them:* they actually were her brothers, though denying it!

—THOMAS CARLYLE

How shall they grasp Thy glory who despise
The law that is Thy Kingdom here on earth,
Our way of freedom and our path to Thee?

He, and he only, in one timeless flash
The inexorable sequences of law,
And, in the self-same flash, transfiguring all,
Uniting and transcending all, beholds . . .
God in the hidden law that fools call "chance,"
God in the star, the flower, the moondrawn wave,
God in the snake, the bird, and the wild beast,
God in the long ascension from the dark,
God in the body and in the soul of man,
God uttering life, and God receiving death.

—ALFRED NOYES

Have we not all one Father?
Hath not one God created us?

—MALACHI 2:10

Making peace ...

Hillel said: Be of the disciples of Aaron, loving peace and pursuing peace, loving thy fellow-creatures, and drawing them near to the Torah.

—ETHICS OF THE FATHERS

My mother has described to me a resplendent person, down on Long Island, whom she knew years ago, in early days. She was known by the name of the Peacemaker. She was well toward eighty years old, of happy and sunny temperament, had always lived on a farm, was very neighborly, sensible and discreet, an invariable and welcomed favorite, especially with young married women. She had numerous children and grandchildren. She was uneducated, but possessed a native dignity. She had come to be a tacitly agreed upon domestic regulator, judge, settler of difficulties, shepherdess, and reconciler in the land.

—WALT WHITMAN

See how great is his reward who makes peace between men. It is written: "Thou shalt build the altar of the Lord thy God of unhewn stones." (Deuteronomy 27:6)
These stones, which cannot hear and cannot see and cannot smell and cannot speak because they make peace between men

through the sacrifices that are offered upon them, the Writ
saves them from the sword and declares:
"Thou shalt lift no iron tool upon them" (Deuteronomy
27:5)—man, who can hear and see and smell and speak—How
much more is this true of him when he makes peace between
his fellow men.

—MIDRASH

Such as have at any time deserved friendship or love
or thanks at my hands, never lost in the same by being no
longer with me. I have better paid and more carefully re-
warded them, being absent and when they least thought of
it. I speake more kindely and affectionately of my friends
when there is least meanes that ever it shall come to their
eares.

—MONTAIGNE

Who is the man that desireth life,
And loveth days, that he may see good therein?
Keep thy tongue from evil,
And thy lips from speaking guile.

—PSALMS 34:13–14

A good man is good even when he is asleep; his character,
which comprises several other factors in addition to mere
habituation, consists in his moral readiness, the wisdom of his
judgment, the sensitiveness with which he can project himself where other selves stand, and the firmness he can show
in defending a vision of right.

—EDMOND CAHN

"Abraham reproved Abimelech." (Genesis 21:25) No friend
is sincere if he withholds corrective rebuke. "Better is open
rebuke than love that is hidden." (Proverbs 29:5) Abraham's
heart-to-heart conversation with Abimelech led to a peaceful
settlement of their difficulties.

—MIDRASH

Love is the divinity who creates peace among men, and calm upon the sea, the windless silence of storms, repose and sleep in sadness.

Love divests us of all alienation from each other, and fills our vacant hearts with overflowing sympathy; he gathers us together in such social meetings as we now delight to celebrate, our guardian and our guide in dances, and sacrifices and feasts.

Yes, Love, who showers benignity on the world, and before whose presence all harsh passions flee and perish; the author of all soft affections; the destroyer of all ungentle thoughts; merciful, mild . . . the father of grace, and delicacy, and gentleness, and delight, and persuasion, and desire; the cherisher of all that is good, the abolisher of all evil; our most excellent pilot, defense, savior and guardian in labor and in fear, in desire and in reason; the ornament and governor of all things human and divine. . . .

—PLATO

An aged man, whom Abraham hospitably invited to his tent, refused to join him in prayer to the one spiritual God. Learning that he was a fire-worshiper, Abraham drove him from his door. That night God appeared to Abraham in a vision and said: "I have borne with that ignorant man for seventy years; could you not have patiently suffered him one night?"

—MIDRASH

When we talk about evil persons this may give rise to evil thoughts, and hence, God forbid, to bringing evil into the world. Therefore, let us talk only about the good ways of righteous men, and so bring good into the world.

—HASIDIC

. . . the complexity of modern civilization is a daily lesson in the necessity of not pressing any claim too far, of understanding opposing points of view, of seeking to reconcile them, of conducting matters so that there is some kind of harmony in a plural society.

—WALTER LIPPMANN

Easily angered and easily appeased—his gain is canceled by
    his loss.
Hard to anger and hard to appease—his loss is canceled by his
    gain.
Hard to anger and easy to appease—the saint.
Easily angered but hard to appease—the wicked.

—ETHICS OF THE FATHERS

I have always believed that the long view of man's history
will show that his destiny on earth is progress toward the
good life, even though that progress is based on sacrifices and
sufferings which taken by themselves seem to constitute a
hideous mélange of evils. This is an act of faith. We must
not let ourselves be engulfed in the passing waves which obscure the current of progress. The sinfulness and weakness
of man are evident to anyone who lives in the active world.
But men are also great, kind and wise. Honor begets honor;
trust begets trust; faith begets faith; and hope is the main-
spring of life.

Those who read this book will mostly be younger than I,
men of the generations who must bear the active part of the
work ahead. Let them charge us with our failures and do
better in their turn. But let them not turn aside from that
which they have to do, nor think that criticism excuses in-
action. Let them have hope, and virtue, and let them believe
in mankind and its future, for there is good as well as evil,
and the man who tries to work for the good, believing in its
eventual victory, while he may suffer setback and even
disaster, will never know defeat. The only deadly sin I know
is cynicism.

—HENRY L. STIMSON

Rabbi Yosi the Galilean says: Great is peace, for even in the
hour of war, we begin in no other way than with "peace."
For it is written: "When you approach a city to fight against
it, then offer peace to it." (Deuteronomy 20:10)

—TALMUD

Societies are renewed—if they are renewed at all—by people who believe in something, care about something, stand for something.

—JOHN W. GARDNER

Rabbi Beroha of Be Hozae was often in the market at Be Lapat. There he would meet Elijah. Once he said to Elijah:

"Is there anyone in this market who shall have the world to come?"

Elijah said to him: "No." . . .

They were standing there when two men came along.

Elijah said to him: "These shall have the world to come."

Rabbi Beroha went to them and said: "What do you do?"

They said to him: "We are jesters and make the sad to laugh. When we see two men quarreling, we strain ourselves to make peace between them."

—TALMUD

The power of an individual...

Rabbi Eliezer, son of Rabbi Simeon, says:
Because the world is judged after its majority,
and man is judged after the majority of his deeds:
if he does one good deed, happy is he, for he has weighted
    the balance in his favor and that of the whole world.
If he commits one transgression, woe is him, for he has
    weighted the balance against him and against the whole
    world.

—TALMUD

... let no man or woman suppose that the smallest social act
of goodness is wasted for society at large. All our help, petty
though it be, is needed; and though we know not the manner, the fruit of every faithful service is surely gathered in.
Let the true and noble words of a great teacher ring in con-
clusion upon our ears: "The growing good of the world is
partly dependent on unhistoric acts; and that things are not
so ill with you and me as they might have been, is half
owing to the number who lived faithfully a hidden life and
rest in unvisited tombs."

—C. G. MONTEFIORE

One person with a belief is a social power equal to ninety-
nine who have only interests.

—JOHN STUART MILL

The world was created only for the sake of choice and of the chooser.

Man, the master of choice, shall say: "Only for my sake was the whole world created!" Therefore every man shall be watchful, and strive to redeem the world and supply that wherein it is lacking, at all times and in all places.

—HASIDIC

A man is the sum of his actions, of what he has *done*, of what he can do. Nothing else.

—ANDRÉ MALRAUX

There is no great thought that has become an impelling power in history which has not been espoused at its origin by men willing to put all their physical and spiritual powers entirely at its service.

—LOUIS GINZBERG

When God wants an important thing done in His World, or a wrong righted, He goes about it in a roundabout fashion. He never lets loose thunderbolts nor stirs up earthquakes. He simply has a tiny baby born.

—MARGARET APPLEGARTH

Man has been given free will: if he wishes to turn toward the good way and to be righteous, the power is in his own hands; if he wishes to turn toward the evil way and to be wicked, the power is likewise in his own hands.

Thus it is written in the Torah: "And the Lord God said, Behold, the man is become as one of us, to know good and evil." (Genesis 3:26) This means that in regard to this matter, the species of man became single of its kind in this world, and that no other species is like it. Man knows good and evil out of himself, out of his intelligence and reason. He does what he wishes to do, and there is none to restrain his hand from doing either good or evil.

—MAIMONIDES

You have not done enough, you have never done enough,
so long as it is still possible that you have something of value
to contribute.

—DAG HAMMARSKJÖLD

A wise man will not leave the right to the mercy of chance,
nor wish it to prevail through the power of the majority.

—HENRY DAVID THOREAU

In the space of time between birth and death, nothing is pre-
determined. You can change everything, you can stop the
war and even maintain peace if you want to do so enough,
intensely and for a long time.

—ALBERT CAMUS

"If you do what is right in God's sight . . ." (Exodus 15:26)
That is, what is right in business, or in buying and selling.
And hence you may learn that he who conducts his business,
and buys and sells in truth and fidelity, and in whom the
mind of man finds pleasure, is regarded as if he fulfilled the
whole law.

—MIDRASH

Even for the sake of *one* righteous man the world would have
been created . . . and for the sake of *one* righteous man it will
continue.

—TALMUD

If the instinct for human survival is atrophying but not yet
dead, where will regeneration come from? It cannot come
from the group, however exalted the purpose of the group
may be. The hope has to reside where it has always been—
with the individual.

—NORMAN COUSINS

Every true man is a cause, a country, and an age; requires
infinite spaces and numbers and time fully to accomplish
his design;—and posterity seems to follow his steps as a train
of clients.

—RALPH WALDO EMERSON

A sceptic approached a famous Rabbi with a plan to embarrass him. He hid a bird in his hand behind his back and then asked: "Rabbi," he said, "I have a bird in my hand. Tell me, is it dead or alive."

If the Rabbi answered "dead," he would let it fly away. If the answer was "alive," he intended to snuff out its life and present the "wise" man with a dead bird.

The Rabbi gave thought for a moment and answered: "My son, the choice of life or death is in your hands!"

—HASIDIC

What men believe is a function of what they are; and what they are is in part what has happened to them.

—WILLIAM GOLDING

There are men who suffer terrible distress and are unable to tell what they feel in their hearts, and they go their way and suffer and suffer. But if they meet one with a laughing face, he can revive them with his joy. And to revive a man is no slight thing.

—HASIDIC

3.WHO DEPRIVES YOU OF YOUR RIGHTS?

Who Deprives You of Your Rights?
You have the *right* to think and speak your mind,

the *right* to have a family,

the *right* to choose where to live,

the *right* to work,

the *right* to a good life,

the *right* to worship God.

We all realize how much these, and many other of our deepest rights, are threatened from many parts of the world today. And we are ready to struggle in every way possible to protect our rights from being taken from us by others.

Yet we don't always see how the security and enjoyment of our rights can be taken from us . . . *by ourselves.*

Let us examine some of the inevitable reasons for this:

There is no way, for example, to enjoy our *right* to a family, without fulfilling our *duty* to care for our children.

For how can anyone expect to get fulfillment and pleasure from his children . . . if they are not raised well?

It is no different with other rights. All experience, history and tradition make clear that no right stands alone.

We can enjoy a right only by accepting the duty which is its other side.

The Right to Think and Speak Our Mind

This is inseparable from our *duty* to *listen;* to give those around us the same rights of expression we want so much for ourselves. When we do not listen, how can we expect others to let us speak?

The Right to Have a Family

We make this right empty and meaningless if we keep postponing the time we spend with our own family. It is a familiar delusion to think that our greatest duty to our family is to provide those we love with material security.

However important this may be, they need our presence and our active love still more.

The Right to Choose Where We Live

Whenever we self-righteously complain and discriminate against our neighbors . . . whenever we fail our *duties* as a good neighbor . . . we undermine the very foundation of our *right* to choose where to live.

The Right to Work

In the complexities of modern society, each of us has the right to earn a living for himself and his family, in ways consistent with his talents. But we fail our duty when we do not give full measure of integrity and effort to whatever we do. And failing this duty, we defeat our right to work.

The Right to a Good Life

No one can "give" us a good life. We are given only the opportunity; there still remain our duty and actions to achieve it. And we advance ourselves whenever we de-

cide to reflect for a time, rather than to keep rushing
through life; whenever we decide to give ourselves to a
community action instead of limiting ourselves to giving
only money; whenever we decide to seek wisdom from
those who can teach us . . . and don't put off the reading
of a book.

The Right to Worship God

We see everywhere how much the evil in human affairs
comes from the tendency to mistake a *part* of life—power
or status or possessions—for the *whole* of it..

We can make the same error in our beliefs. For our right
to worship God is also our duty not to fall into the
idolatry of worshiping any *part* of His creation as though
it were the *whole*.

*It is clear, then, that to enjoy our rights we must fulfill
our duties.*

They are the only path to the full possession of our rights.
Moreover, each individual's *rights* are insured only when
we achieve a society where all are concerned with their
duties.

And *only* then!

You can enjoy a right
only by doing your <u>duty</u>...

A duty is the other side
of a right...

A man must perform his duty to his fellows exactly as to
the Omnipresent . . .

Whence is it derived? . . . "So that thou shalt find favor and
good understanding in the sight of God and man." (Proverbs
3:4)

—MISHNAH

In a century in which so many of the mentors of the public
mind—from the psychiatrists to the ad-men—speak to us in
terms of "what we owe to ourselves," may there not indeed
have been a slackening of devotion compared with those
days, not so long distant, when what man owes to God and
his neighbor was a common theme of public discourse?

—ADLAI E. STEVENSON

It is related that a wagon-driver came to Rabbi Akiba and
said to him: "Rabbi, teach me the whole Torah at once."
He replied: "My son, Moses our teacher stayed on the Mount
forty days and forty nights before he learned it, and you
want me to teach you the whole of it at once! Still, my son,
this is the basic principle of the Torah: What is hateful to
yourself, do not do to your fellow-man. If you do not want

others to harm what belongs to you, do not harm what belongs to another; if you do not want others to take from you what is yours, do not take from another what is his."

The man rejoined his companions and they journeyed until they came to a field full of seed-pods. His companions took two, but he took none. They continued on their journey, and came to a field full of cabbages. They each took two, but he took none.

They asked him why he had not taken any, and he replied: "Thus did Rabbi Akiba teach me: What is hateful to yourself, do not to your fellow-man. If you wish that nobody should take from you what is yours, do not take from another what is his."

—FATHERS ACCORDING TO RABBI NATHAN

Man finds the meaning of his human existence in his capacity for decision, in his freedom of choice. It is a dreadful freedom, for it also means responsibility, but without it man would be as nothing.

—WILL HERBERG

Not everyone in chains is subdued; at times, a chain is greater than a necklace.

—KAHLIL GIBRAN

I the Lord search the heart,
I try the reins,
Even to give every man according to his ways,
According to the fruit of his doings.

—JEREMIAH 17:10

I have now spoken of the education of the scholar . . . It remains to say somewhat of his duties.

. . . He is one who raises himself from private considerations and breathes and lives on public and illustrious thoughts. He is the world's eye. He is the world's heart. He is to resist the vulgar prosperity that retrogrades ever to barbarism, by preserving and communicating heroic sentiments, noble biographies, melodious verse, and the conclusions of history.

—RALPH WALDO EMERSON

. . . the son shall not bear the iniquity of the father with him, neither shall the father bear the iniquity of the son with him; the righteousness of the righteous shall be upon him, and the wickedness of the wicked shall be upon him.

—EZEKIEL 18:20

Freedom is an indivisible word. If we want to enjoy it, and fight for it, we must be prepared to extend it to everyone.

—WENDELL L. WILLKIE

It never occurs to us that this irreverence for the past, this perpetual battering away at institutions considered sacred by the great majority of mankind, this worship of individualism which in most cases is nothing more than thinly disguised selfishness and vanity, and this disregard of authority and the utter absence of the qualities of submission and obedience are, in part at least, responsible for the rampant materialism and unrighteousness which we all so much deplore.

—SOLOMON SCHECHTER

It is as though a man went into a shop, and asked for a pint of wine. The shopkeeper says to him, "Give me your vessel." But the man opens his bag.

Then he says to the shopkeeper, "Give me some oil." When the shopkeeper asks for the vessel, he offers the corner of his garment.

The shopkeeper says to him: "You have not got a vessel, and yet you want to buy wine and oil."

So God says to the wicked: You are destitute of good deeds, yet you want to learn Torah? . . . As it is written: "But unto the wicked God saith, 'What hast thou to do to declare My statutes.' " (Psalms 50:16)

—FATHERS ACCORDING TO RABBI NATHAN

. . . the goal of human effort is to be able . . . to follow what the heart desires without transgressing what is right.

—WALTER LIPPMANN

The law that manifests itself to the eyes of man everywhere—
in the blade of grass which completes its course in unfolding
and withering, in the stone that falls to earth, in the track of
the stars far above us—this same law rules the life of man,
and the same God whose law is obeyed by the entire universe
in its tiniest parts, gave also to man the law of his life.

—LOUIS GINZBERG

The talkative listen to no one, for they are ever speaking.
And the first evil that attends those who know not how to
be silent is that they hear nothing.

—PLUTARCH

The worker is not permitted to work at night and then to
hire himself out again during the day. He also should not go
hungry or afflict himself because this is stealing the work of
the employer. [The worker will be inefficient.]

—TALMUD

Who is worthy of honor? He who respects his fellow-men;
as it is said: "For them that honor Me I will honor, and they
that despise Me shall be lightly esteemed." (I Samuel 2:30)

—ETHICS OF THE FATHERS

The obstacles to fulfilling
one's duty...

The Evil Inclination is like one who runs about the world keeping his hand closed. Nobody knows what he has inside of it. He goes up to everyone and asks: "What do you suppose I have in my hand?" And every person thinks that just what he wants most of all is hidden there. And everyone runs after the Evil Inclination. Then he opens his hand, it is empty.

—HASIDIC

One man's duty may differ from another's and what is good at one time may not be the right thing at another time. Unselfishness and unbroken reliance on God and faithful use of one's reasoning powers must decide what at each juncture, public or private, one's duty is.

—CHAKRAVARTI RAJAGOPALACHARI

The style of conduct which carries weight calls for stubbornness even in an act of concession: you have to be severe with yourself in order to have the right to be gentle to others.

—DAG HAMMARSKJÖLD

If . . . duty is not filled with good-will and desire, it is morally hateful, or at very best, a necessary evil—one of those compromises with the world which must be made in order to get through it at all.

—RANDOLPH BOURNE

We thought the tragedy was that the possible was impossible. The impossible is possible. That's the tragedy.

—ELIE WIESEL

The real moral peril consists not so much in choosing what in our best judgment seems to be the lesser evil; such choice is entailed by the very process of living. The real moral peril consists in trying to make a virtue out of necessity, in converting the lesser evil we choose, merely because we choose it, into a positive good.

—WILL HERBERG

The Words of the Law are comparable to a medicine of life. Like a king, who inflicted a wound upon his son, and then bandaged the wound. He said, "My son, so long as this bandage is on your wound, eat and drink what you like, and wash in cold or warm water, and you will suffer no harm. If you remove it, it will become infected."

So God says, "I created in you the evil inclination, but I created the Law as a medicine. As long as you occupy yourselves with the Law, the evil inclination will not rule over you. But if you do not occupy yourselves with the Torah, then you will be delivered into the power of the evil inclination, and it will harm you."

—TALMUD

. . . men yield their greatest product when they have confidence in the order of life of which they are a part . . . morale is as important as money and materials and machines.

—ARTHUR G. COONS

When the props beneath an edifice rot away, it does not fall immediately. The decay is likely to be gradual, and slower in some areas than in others. Again, the building may hold together by inertia and the interweaving of its parts. But ultimately, a collapse must come. This, there is reason to believe, is what we are now undergoing: a moral breakdown consequent on the disintegration in modern man of religious faith.

—MILTON STEINBERG

The fact that reason is rare in reality and always imperfect, even among philosophers, shows that man's way is hard, not that it is impossible.

—KARL JASPERS

[We] . . . confused the free with the free and easy.

—ADLAI E. STEVENSON

The most dangerous of all moral dilemmas: when we are obliged to conceal truth in order to help the truth to be victorious. If this should at any time become our duty in the role assigned us by fate, how strait must be our path at all times, if we are not to perish.

—DAG HAMMARSKJÖLD

One day a hasid came to the Rabbi; he was rich, but a miser. The Rabbi took him by the hand and led him to the window. "Look out there," he said. And the rich man looked into the street.
"What do you see?" asked the Rabbi.
"People," answers the rich man. Again the Rabbi takes him by the hand, and this time leads him to the mirror.
"What do you see now?" he says. "Now I see myself," answers the rich man.
Then the Rabbi says: "Behold—in the window there is glass, and in the mirror there is glass. But the glass of the mirror is covered with a little silver, and no sooner is the silver added than you cease to see others but see only yourself."

—S. ANSKY

[Hillel] used to say: An empty-headed man cannot be a sinfearing man, nor can an ignorant person be pious, the timid cannot learn, the short-tempered cannot teach; he who is mostly occupied with business will not grow wise, and where there are no men, strive to be a man.

—ETHICS OF THE FATHERS

We are too pragmatic. We demand the short-term result and are often too impatient to explore its later consequences. We like to define things in precise terms, and the definition betrays us into fixed positions from which we cannot withdraw.

—MORRIS L. WEST

He who is ever brooding over results often loses nerve in the performance of duty. He becomes impatient and then gives vent to anger and begins to do unworthy things; he jumps from action to action, never remaining faithful to any.

—MAHATMA GANDHI

If your heart does not *want* a world of moral reality, your head will assuredly never make you believe in one.

—WILLIAM JAMES

Rabbi Judah taught: Study the Law and do good deeds, even if not for its own sake. For through being occupied with the Law, even if not for its own sake, you will come to fulfill it for its own sake.

—TALMUD

Fulfillment comes with
the performance of one's duty...

Rabbi Hanina, the son of Dosa, said: He whose deeds exceed his wisdom, his wisdom shall endure; but he whose wisdom exceeds his deeds, his wisdom will not endure.

—ETHICS OF THE FATHERS

... individuals must give up a share of liberty to preserve the rest.

—ANDREW JACKSON

Question: Why is it written: "In the day that God created *a man* on earth" (Genesis 5:1), and not "in the day that God created *man* on earth"?

Answer: You shall serve your Creator as if there were only one man in the world, only you yourself.

—HASIDIC

The motto of life is: "Give and Take." Everyone must be both a giver and a receiver. Who is not both is as a barren tree.

—HASIDIC

Isn't the fulfillment of our duty towards our neighbor an expression of our deepest desire?

—DAG HAMMARSKJÖLD

. . . sometimes, because of unique combinations of circumstances surrounding him, an individual is indispensable for a
specific role in history. . . . Moses was one of the great spiritual leaders of mankind. He could neglect his duty, but he
could not assign it to anyone else.

—LOUIS FINKELSTEIN

Let us have faith that right makes might; and in that faith
let us to the end, dare to do our duty . . .

—ABRAHAM LINCOLN

Look to the things of God.
Know you are bound to help all who are wronged,
Bound to constrain all who destroy the law.
What else holds state to state save this alone,
That each one honors the great laws of right.

—EURIPIDES

It is better for the health of the soul to make one man good
than "to sacrifice oneself for mankind." For a mature man,
these are not alternatives, but two aspects of self-realization,
which mutually support each other, both being the outcome
of one and the same choice.

—DAG HAMMARSKJÖLD

Shall men, then, always walk in meekness? Not so, say the
Masters. There are moments when haughtiness becomes a
duty. When the Evil Inclination approaches, whispering in
the ear: "You are unworthy to fulfill the Law," say: "I am
worthy."

—HASIDIC

Accomplishment is absolute, not relative. There are no miti-
gating circumstances. Let a man do first-class work or let him
shovel coals.

—THOMAS MANN

It is not why I suffer that I wish to know; but only whether
I suffer for Your sake.

—HASIDIC

> The law of the Lord is perfect, restoring the soul;
> The testimony of the Lord is sure, making wise the simple.
> The precepts of the Lord are right, rejoicing the heart;
> The commandment of the Lord is pure, enlightening the eyes.
> The fear of the Lord is clean, enduring for ever;
> The ordinances of the Lord are true, they are righteous
>   altogether;
> More to be desired are they than gold, yea, than much fine
>   gold;
> Sweeter also than honey and the honeycomb.
>
> —PSALMS 19:8–11

We must come to an understanding—with ourselves, and with
others. This involves the fourth dimension of Man. The first
three we know: Man's needs for food, for clothing, and for
shelter. The fourth is more elusive; it concerns Man's fulfillment. Man aspires to something he can never fully achieve.

—EDWARD M. KEATING

> Science says things are; morality says some things are better
> than other things; and religion says . . . that the best things
> are the more eternal things . . .
>
> —WILLIAM JAMES

The judge who does not agonize before passing sentence is
a criminal.

—JOHN CIARDI

> There are three crowns, the crown of Law (the Torah), the
> crown of the Priesthood, and the crown of the Kingdom.
> Aaron was worthy of the crown of the Priesthood and ob-
> tained it. David was worthy of the crown of the Kingdom
> and obtained it. The crown of the Torah remains, so that no

man shall have the pretext to say: "If the crown of the Priesthood and the crown of the Kingdom were yet available, I would have proven myself worthy of them and have obtained them."

For the crown of the Law is available to all. As God says: "Of him who proves himself worthy of that crown, I reckon it to him as if all the three were yet available, and he had proven himself worthy of them all. And if everyone who does not prove himself worthy of the crown of the Law, I reckon it unto him as if all three were yet available, and he had proved himself worthy of none of them."

—MIDRASH

Rights are insured in a society when all are concerned with their duties...

Understanding another's feelings, thoughts, needs...

Hillel says: Do not withdraw from the community. . . . Do not judge your comrade until you have stood in his place.
—ETHICS OF THE FATHERS

You can only hope to find a lasting solution to a conflict if you have learned to see the other objectively, but, at the same time, to experience his difficulties subjectively.
—DAG HAMMARSKJÖLD

Rabbi Moshe Leib of Sassov declared to his disciples: "I have learned how we must truly love our neighbor from a conversation between two villagers which I overheard.

The first said: 'Tell me, friend Ivan, do you love me?'
The second: 'I love you deeply.'
The first: 'Do you know, my friend, what gives me pain?'
The second: 'How can I, pray, know what gives you pain?'
The first: 'If you do not know what gives me pain, how can you say that you truly love me?'

"Understand, then, my sons," continued the Sassover, "to love, truly to love, means to know what brings pain to your comrade."
—HASIDIC

Disinterestedness is a necessary attribute to real friendship and it is the duty of one friend to guess another's problems and render assistance before it is asked. If our friends have needs that we can satisfy, we should relieve them of the necessity of seeking our help. Apart from the satisfaction usually produced by an action, this permanent ability to give pleasure is perhaps the only advantage of wealth and power.

—ANDRÉ MAUROIS

The brotherhood is not by the blood certainly:
But neither are men brothers by speech—by saying so:
Men are brothers by life lived and are hurt for it:

Hunger and hurt are the great begetters of brotherhood:
Humiliation has gotten much love:
Danger I say is the nobler father and mother . . .

—ARCHIBALD MACLEISH

Ben Azzai used to say: Hold no man insignificant and no thing improbable, for there is no man who has not his hour and there is no thing that has not its place.

—ETHICS OF THE FATHERS

Nature hath made men so equall, in the faculties of body, and mind; as that though there bee found one man some-times manifestly stronger in body, or of quicker mind than another; yet when all is reckoned together, the difference between man, and man, is not so considerable, as that one man can thereupon claim to himselfe any benefit, to which another may not pretend, as well as he.

—THOMAS HOBBES

Whoever prays on behalf of a fellowman, while himself being in need of the same thing, will be answered first.

—TALMUD

Rabbi Yosi says: "Let thy fellow's property be as dear to you as your own. . . ."
How so? This teaches that even as one has regard for his own property, so should he have regard for his fellow's property; and even as no man wishes that his own property be held in ill repute, so should he wish that his fellow's property shall not be held in ill repute.

—FATHERS ACCORDING TO RABBI NATHAN

I love you because you are weak before the strong oppressor, and poor before the greedy rich. For these reasons I shed tears and comfort you; and from behind my tears I see you embraced in the arms of Justice, smiling and forgiving your persecutors. You are my brother and I love you.

—KAHLIL GIBRAN

There may be moments in friendship, as in love, when silence is beyond words. The faults of our friend may be clear to us, but it is well to seem to shut our eyes to them. Friendship is usually treated by the majority of mankind as a tough and everlasting thing which will survive all manner of bad treatment. But this is an exceedingly great and foolish error; it may die in an hour of a single unwise word; its conditions of existence are that it should be dealt with delicately and tenderly, being as it is a sensitive plant and not a roadside thistle. We must not expect our friend to be above humanity.

—OUIDA

In these days, it is doubtful that any child may reasonably be expected to succeed in life if he is denied the opportunity of an education. Such an opportunity, where the state has undertaken to provide it, is a right which must be made available to all on equal terms.

—EARL WARREN

A friend whom you have been enjoying during your whole life, you ought not to be displeased with in a moment. A stone is many years becoming a ruby; take care that you do not destroy it in an instant against another stone.

—SAADI

. . . What is a friend? Someone who for the first time makes you aware of your loneliness and his, and helps you to escape so you in turn can help him. Thanks to him you can hold your tongue without shame and talk freely without risk. That's it.

—ELIE WIESEL

. . . judge everyone with the scale weighted in his favor.

—ETHICS OF THE FATHERS

Man's dependence on
his fellow-man...

Ben Zoma said: How hard the first man, Adam, must have labored before he could eat a bit of bread! He had to plough and sow and weed and hoe and reap and thresh, winnow and sift, grind, sift again, knead, moisten and bake, and only after all this eat his bread; whereas I get up in the morning and find the bread all ready for me.

What toil Adam had till he could be clothed with the simplest raiment! He had to shear, bleach, beat the wool, dye it, spin it, weave it, wash it, and sew it together, and only after all this was he clothed; whereas I get up in the morning, and find all my clothes prepared for me.

How many workmen get up early, and go late to rest! Whereas I get up in the morning, and find all the things I need before me.

—TALMUD

Man is not a farmer, or a professor, or an engineer, but he is all. Man is priest, and scholar, and statesman, and producer, and soldier. In the *divided* or social state these functions are parceled out to individuals, each of whom aims to do his stint of the joint work, whilst each other performs his . . . the individual, to possess himself, must sometimes return from his own labor to embrace all the other laborers.

—RALPH WALDO EMERSON

How does a man find his Father who is in heaven?
He finds him by good deeds, and study of the Torah.
And the Holy One, blessed be He, finds man
through love, through brotherhood, through respect,
through companionship, through truth, through peace,
through bending the knee, through humility,
through studious session, through commerce lessened,
through the service of the masters, through discussion of
    students,
through a good heart, through decency,
through No that is really No,
through Yes that is really Yes.

—MIDRASH

. . . no law can require us to be our brother's keeper, as
individual citizens or as a nation. But ethically, we do care.
I believe that this deeper, ethical concern is ingrained in most
Americans. It is latent within us, as part of our national
character.

—ARTHUR J. GOLDBERG

This was Rabbi Mihal's comment on the words of Hillel,
"If I am not for myself, who will be for me? And if I am
for myself, what am I?" (Ethics of the Fathers 1:14)

" 'If I am not for myself,' that is, if I do not work for myself
alone, but continually participate in the congregation, 'who
will be for me?' In that case, whatever 'who,' that is, whatever any member of the congregation does in my place
counts just as though I had done it myself. But if I am 'for
myself'—if I do not participate with others, if I do not join
with them—'what am I?' Then everything in the way of
good works which I have wrought alone is less than nothing
in the eyes of God, who is the source of all good."

—HASIDIC

Our American heritage . . . teaches that to be secure in the
rights he wishes for himself, each man must be willing to
respect the rights of other men.

—PRESIDENT'S COMMITTEE ON CIVIL RIGHTS

When man quits the world, he is asked, according to an ancient Midrash, "Hast thou been busy in the study of the Torah, and in works of lovingkindness? Hast thou declared thy Maker as King morning and evening? Hast thou acknowledged thy fellow-man as king over thee in meekness of spirit?" Man should accordingly perceive in his fellow-man not only an equal whose rights he is bound to respect, but a superior whom he is obliged to revere and love. In every person, it is pointed out by these saints, precious and noble elements are latent, not to be found with anybody else.

—SOLOMON SCHECHTER

You have four children and I [God] have four children. Your four children are your son, your daughter, manservant and maid. My [God's] four children are the Levite, the stranger, the widow and the orphan. You provide for and make my four children happy, and I will make your four children rejoice.

—MIDRASH

The Rabbi of Apt said to God: "Lord of the world, I know that I have no virtue and no merit for which, after my death, you could set me in paradise among the righteous. But if you are thinking of putting me in hell among the evil-doers, please remember that I cannot get along with them. So I beg of you to take all the wicked out of hell, so you can put me in."

—HASIDIC

Everything of value in our lives stems from our moving *outward*. Perhaps it is the life force in us exploding as the universe is said to have exploded. We come alive when we feel love. Without it, we have no real access to others, no means of true contact, no awareness of anything except ourselves—perhaps not even of ourselves.

—SARAH PATTON BOYLE

The central theme in our American heritage is the importance of the individual person. From the earliest moment of our history we have believed that every human being has an essential dignity and integrity which must be respected and safeguarded. . . .

Thus, the aspirations and achievements of each member of our society are to be limited only by the skills and energies he brings to the opportunities equally offered to all Americans. We can tolerate no restrictions upon the individual which depend upon irrelevant factors such as his race, his color, his religion or the social position to which he is born.

—PRESIDENT'S COMMITTEE ON CIVIL RIGHTS

Waters boasted they could flood the earth.
Rebuked by God: "Sands will raise up a barrier against you."
Waters ridiculed the thought of small grains of sand standing
    against the mighty waves.
Sands: "True we are each of us by ourselves insignificant,
    but united we can raise barriers forming mounds, hills
    and mountains."
The great army of sands, united, frightened the waters which
    then retreated.

—MIDRASH

Probably, the most dominant theme of our philosophy is cooperation. We have seen competition and we know where it has led the world. We believe in the family of man, and a family cooperates. Those who need help get it; those who have help to give grant it.

—EDWARD M. KEATING

How many things are there which a man cannot, with any face or comeliness, say or do himself; a man can scarce allege his own merits with modesty, much less extol them; a man cannot sometimes brook to supplicate, or beg, and a number of the like: but all these things are graceful in a friend's mouth, which are blushing in a man's own. So again, a man's person hath many proper relations which he cannot put off.

A man cannot speak to his son but as a father; to his wife but as a husband; to his enemy but upon terms: whereas a friend may speak as the case requires, and not as it sorteth with the person: but to enumerate these things were endless; I have given the rule, where a man cannot fitly play his own part, if he have not a friend he may quit the stage.

—FRANCIS BACON

Now, take the history of the world, search the annals of our race, and see for yourself whether this greatest of all miracles, the conversion of a community to righteousness, or even the regeneration of a single individual, was ever effected by oratory alone, or rather by the saintly men who sacrificed . . . their very lives in the service of ideas and ideals.

—SOLOMON SCHECHTER

In Germany, the Nazis first came for the Communists, and I didn't speak up because I was not a Communist. Then they came for the Jews, and I did not speak up because I was not a Jew. Then they came for the Trade Unionists, and I didn't speak up because I wasn't a Trade Unionist.

Then they came for ME . . . by that time there was no one to speak up for anyone.

—MARTIN NIEMOELLER

A favorite saying of the masters of Yavneh was:
I am God's creature and my fellow man is God's creature.
My work is in the city and his work is in the field.
I rise early to go to my work, and he rises early to go to his work.
As he does not pride himself on his work, so I do not pride myself on mine.
But should you think that I am doing more than he—
we have learned:
"Do more, do less, it matters not, so long as one's heart is turned to heaven."

—TALMUD

Justice is the basis of
community peace...

Rabbi Simeon, son of Gamliel, said: By three things is the world sustained: by truth, by justice, and by peace, as it is said, "Truth and justice and peace judge you in your gates." (Zechariah 8:16)

—ETHICS OF THE FATHERS

The three [justice, truth, peace] are really one; if justice is executed, truth is vindicated, and peace results.

—TALMUD

Thou shalt not wrest judgment; thou shalt not respect persons; neither shalt thou take a gift; for a gift doth blind the eyes of the wise, and pervert the words of the righteous. Justice, justice shalt thou follow, that thou mayest live, and inherit the land which the Lord thy God giveth thee.

—DEUTERONOMY 16:19–20

Where the city stands with the brawniest breed of orators
    and bards;
Where the city stands that is beloved by these, and loves
    them in return, and understands them;

Where no monuments exist to heroes, but in the common
   words and deeds;
Where thrift is in its place, and prudence is in its place;

· · ·

Where the slave ceases, and the master of slaves ceases;
Where the populace rise at once against the never-ending
   audacity of elected persons;
Where fierce men and women pour forth, as the sea to the
   whistle of death pours its sweeping and unript waves;
Where outside authority enters always after the precedence
   of inside authority;

· · ·

Where equanimity is illustrated in affairs;
Where speculations on the Soul are encouraged;

· · ·

Where the city of the faithfulest friends stands;
Where the city of the cleanliness of the sexes stands;
Where the city of the healthiest fathers stands;
Where the city of the best-bodied mothers stands,
There the great city stands.

—WALT WHITMAN

> Nay, but if ye thoroughly amend your ways and your do-
> ings; if ye thoroughly execute justice between a man and his
> neighbor; if ye oppress not the stranger, the fatherless, and
> the widow, and shed not innocent blood in this place, neither
> walk after other gods to your hurt; then will I cause you
> to dwell in this place, in the land that I gave to your fathers,
> for ever and ever.

—JEREMIAH 7:5–7

Justice no man has seen, nor shall see. Yet what is man's
political life without it? The useless becomes the worthful.
Beauty no man has seen, nor shall see. Yet what is man's
whole artistic aspiration without it? The useless becomes the
worthful. *Truth* no man has seen, nor shall see. Yet what
is science without it? The useless becomes the worthful.
Holiness no man hath seen, nor shall see. Yet where is religion without it? The useless becomes the worthful.

—T. V. SMITH

Rabbi Banaah began [his sermon]: "False scales are an abomination of the Lord." (Proverbs 11:1) If you see a generation
whose weights are false, know that the government will
quarrel with that generation [persecute it]. From whence do
we derive this? It is written, "False scales are an abomination
of the Lord" and afterwards it is written, "When wickedness
cometh, then cometh shame." (Proverbs 11:2)

—MIDRASH

. . . if the abuse be enormous, Nature will rise up, and claim-
ing her original rights, overturn a corrupt political system.

—SAMUEL JOHNSON

Justice is the soil in which all the other virtues can prosper.
It is the pre-condition of all social virtue, indeed of all community life. It makes civilized existence, it makes human
existence possible. In every society justice must be the para-
mount concern, for it is the very foundation of all society:
"Let justice roll down like waters, and righteousness as a
mighty stream." (Amos 5:24)

—SHALOM SPIEGEL

Law expresses the political and philosophical ideas of a people. It can make life oppressive or it can make life free. In a
democracy, the function of law is to guarantee order and
justice. Law can preserve order without justice or dispense
justice without order. But without both order and justice
the democratic ideals of free ballot, free speech, free worship
and fair trial cannot be achieved.

—FRANK E. HORACK, JR.

The Holy One, blessed be He, continued to appease Moses.
He said to him:
"Am I not your Father, and you my children,
you my brothers, and I your brother;
you my friends, and I your friend;
you my lovers, and I your lover?
Have I allowed you to lack?

All that I ask you is this, as I have examined myself and
  found eleven qualities [of virtue].
So all I ask of you is [these] eleven qualities.
And they are:
'He that walketh uprightly, and worketh righteousness,
And speaketh truth in his heart;
That hath not slander upon his tongue,
Nor doeth evil to his fellow.
Nor taketh up a reproach against his neighbor;
In whose eyes a vile person is despised,
But he honoreth them that fear the Lord;
He that sweareth to his own hurt, and changeth not;
He that putteth not out his money on interest,
Nor taketh a bribe against the innocent,
He that doeth these things shall never be moved.' " (Psalms
  15:2–5)
The Holy One, blessed be He, continued to appease Moses.
He said to him:
"Do I at all favor an Israelite or a Gentile, a man or a woman,
  a man-servant or a maid-servant?
But whoever he is who keeps a commandment, the reward is
  at its heels."
Hence it was said:
He who honors heaven more, heaven's honor is more, and his
  own honor is more, as well.
He who honors heaven less, and honors himself more, heav-
  en's honor continues the same, but his own honor is less.

—MIDRASH

The public good is in nothing more essentially interested
than in the protection of every individual's private rights.

—SIR WILLIAM BLACKSTONE

Where there is ignorance you must bring knowledge, where
there is poverty, you must bring relief, and, most important,
where there is oppression, you must bring justice.

—EDWARD M. KEATING

Certain ancient rules apply with equal force to Jew and Christian, atheist and agnostic, to all men in all situations. These immutable laws are expressed in various ways. The Pentateuch reveals the Decalogue and the Golden Rule of Leviticus 19:18: "Thou shalt love thy neighbor as thyself" . . .

Yet these and other binding commandments are often violated in the American business community. A man fears he may be risking his business if he obeys them, forgetting, however, that if he violates them he risks the world.

—LOUIS FINKELSTEIN

> Raba said:
> When a man is led in to be judged [in the next world] he
>   is asked:
> Have you done your business reliably?
> Have you set yourself regular periods to study?
> Have you begotten children?
> Have you looked forward to redemption?
> Have you used all your wits in the study of the law?
> Have you understood how one thing will follow from an-
>   other?
> Yet even so—if "the fear of the Lord is his treasure" (Isaiah
>   33:6), it will go well with him; if not, it will not.
>
> —TALMUD

4. WHERE DOES THE WORLD START?

Where Does the World Start?

. . . at your fingertips!

Do you say:

"There's nothing I can do about the problems of the world."

Nothing?

This is a common mistake, for there isn't a world problem which does not begin where you are.

And always you can diminish or add to it.

Not to be aware of this—not knowing the difference you make—is in itself one of the biggest of world problems.

Consider these three major issues of our time:

Ignorance
Poverty
Oppression

We often think the world problem is *ignorance*.

Yet the real problem is our unwillingness to learn.

In talking to our family, to our neighbors, to business associates or to the peoples of the world, we're often so busy thinking of *answers* to give them, we don't really hear what they have to say to us.

We want to teach when our need is to learn.

No one can fight ignorance this way. Only when we're ready to listen to others can we hope they will learn with us and from us.

When we do this, when we concern ourselves with listening and learning, we diminish ignorance in the world, right where we are.

We often think the world problem is *poverty*.

Yet the real problem is our short-sightedness.

We tend to believe the best way to secure our well-being is to accumulate more and more goods, even if this is at the expense of others.

That is no more than an animal does.

And the long history of man has shown repeatedly that ethical wisdom and practical wisdom point to the same truth:

No one surrounded by poverty can be rich.

Certainly, no accumulation of possessions can preserve our well-being, except when those around us share in our wealth, too.

The man willing to share his responsibilities and his opportunities to create wealth can never be crushed by them. And he does not find his security undermined by the needs and hungers of others.

We can be sure that to share what we have will reduce poverty in the world, right where we are.

We often think the world problem is *oppression*.

Yet the real problem is the rejection of our neighbors.

We see people all around us trying, in their pride, to lift themselves up, not by their own growth but by lowering others.

They engage in an endless, empty attempt to raise their status by leaving others out.

And sometimes we find ourselves among them.

Here, too, we fail to recognize how much the ideal and the practical are the same.

For the simple fact is: Each of us belongs inalienably to the Family of Man. There are no strangers left on earth.

We are all alike in that each of us is different, yet all of us are neighbors.

That's why we have the power to reduce oppression in the world. We do so whenever we welcome a neighbor of whatever race or creed or color; whenever we make him feel at home in our community.

This is where the world starts.

We must understand how much we can do in the world in yet another way.

We not only receive the world from the generations of the past. We also pass it on to those who come after us.

And we are descendants of great men who recognize their obligations to fight ignorance, poverty and oppression everywhere.

We must do no less.

For we are a generation to whom greatness of heritage and opportunity have been given.

So each of us faces these questions:

How shall we pass on our inheritance: Will it be diminished or increased?

Will we be the *grandfathers* . . . or only the *grandsons* of great men?

This is why it was said:

"God *of* Abraham, God *of* Isaac, God *of* Jacob" (Prayer Book) and not "God of Abraham, Isaac and Jacob."

It was to let each generation know that, while we inherit a tradition, we must still achieve our own understanding and meet our own responsibilities in what we owe to life and God.

To reduce ignorance...

Self-examination...

A man cannot find redemption until he sees the flaws in his soul, and tries to efface them. Nor can a people be redeemed until it sees the flaws in its soul and tries to efface them. But whether it be a man or a people, whoever shuts out the realization of his flaws is shutting out redemption. We can be redeemed only to the extent to which we see ourselves.

—HASIDIC

My strength is as the strength of ten,
Because my heart is pure.
—ALFRED, LORD TENNYSON

Around a man who has been pushed into the limelight, a legend begins to grow as it does around a dead man. But a dead man is in no danger of yielding to the temptation to nourish his legend, or accept its picture as reality. I pity the man who falls in love with his image as it is drawn by public opinion during the honeymoon of publicity.

—DAG HAMMARSKJÖLD

. . . maybe everyone should begin self-examination at home. Do you and I have this faith to the limit? If the answer is yes, and I think it is, if we have this faith to the limit, that's all we can do, plus say so. We should say so whenever we can, and wherever we can.

. . . I don't think it's a question of what other people think; more importantly it's what we think. And maybe that's what saves the society: every member in it looking within himself and saying, "Who am I? What do *I* think?" Not, "What does my neighbor think?" . . .

—MARK VAN DOREN

Words of Torah are like golden vessels, the more you scour them and rub them, the more they glisten and reflect the face of him who looks at them. So with the words of Torah, whenever you repeat them, they glisten and lighten the face, as it says, "The Commandment of the Lord is pure, enlightening the eyes." (Psalms 9:9) But if you neglect them, they become like vessels of glass which are easily broken, as it says, "Gold and glass cannot be put side by side." (Job 28:17) The gold and the crystal cannot equal it, that is, equal wisdom.

—FATHERS ACCORDING TO RABBI NATHAN

Solitude gives birth to the original in us, to beauty unfamiliar and perilous . . .

—THOMAS MANN

Make it thy business to know thyself, which is the most difficult lesson in the world.

—MIGUEL DE CERVANTES

My experience has been that what the thoroughly educated man doubted first and last was *his* own infallibility.

—SOLOMON SCHECHTER

. . . the true value of souls is in proportion to what they can admire . . .

—WALTER PATER

The Lord! The Lord! That means: I am one and the same merciful God before a man sins and after he sins.

Maharsha of blessed memory raised the question: What need does a man have of mercy before he sins?

There is, however, an account in the book *Duties of the Heart*, of a certain righteous man who said to his disciples: If there were no sin in you, I would have fear in your behalf of something that is worse than sin, and that is pride. For he who believes that he has not sinned has pride within himself, and that is worse than sin. And thus before a man sins he is certainly in need of mercy to gain forgiveness for the pride in his heart.

—HASIDIC

The first question written on the blackboard was, "Which of the required readings in this course did you find least interesting?" Then, after members of the class had had ten minutes in which to expatiate on what was certainly to many a congenial topic, he wrote the second question: "To what defect in yourself do you attribute this lack of interest?"

—JOSEPH WOOD KRUTCH

It is ignorance of one's own errors that makes one ready to see the errors of others.

—SOLOMON SCHECHTER

. . . there are many ways to offend against truth. One way is simply to deny it: the way of the liar. . . . Another is to keep silence when the truth should be spoken: the way of the coward. . . . At the other end is the cruel use of truth, which involves harshly and unfeelingly proclaiming the truth when silence is clearly the better part: the way of the oaf or of the insensitive True Believer who has too little concern for other people and too much for his own cause. Another assault on truth, common enough, is made by twisting, distorting, and holding back the little truths in order to serve the large, capital "T" Truth. Here is the way of the propagandist: the man who lies for Truth. . . .

. . . we should be constantly scrutinizing our consciences against these abuses and misuses.

—JOHN COGLEY

It requires age and cooling down to get a little humility. Many a thing which in my youth I considered a humiliation, I look upon now as natural and fair.

—SOLOMON SCHECHTER

The world is his who can see through its pretension. What deafness, what stone-blind custom, what overgrown error you behold, is there only by sufferance—by your sufferance. See it to be a lie, and you have already dealt it its mortal blow.

—RALPH WALDO EMERSON

The first step in the ethical life is self-criticism. As the Talmud puts it, "Cleanse yourselves, and then cleanse others." Ethics is a branch of thought starting with self-discipline.

—LOUIS FINKELSTEIN

The capacity for self-control, the ability to master one's sinful impulses and deal with them constructively, is itself a crucial moral power.

—WILL HERBERG

. . . be rather a tail to lions than a head to foxes.

—ETHICS OF THE FATHERS

We cannot afford to wait with our health until we know the final truth about our bodies and minds.

Neither can we afford to wait with our ethical and spiritual health until we know the ultimate truth about the world and God.

—MORDECAI M. KAPLAN

Embrace not the opacous and blind side of Opinions . . .

—SIR THOMAS BROWNE

Everyone must have two pockets, so that he can reach into the one or the other, according to his needs. In his right pocket are to be the words: "For my sake was the world created," and in his left: "I am dust and ashes."

—HASIDIC

Learning from everyone
and everything...

"They [the sayings of the wise] are given from one shepherd." (Ecclesiastes 12:11) The Holy One, blessed be He, said: "If an ordinary person tells you something and you derive spiritual delight from his insight, regard it as something you heard from a scholar. Moreover, you must even regard it as having been told you by a great sage. And even more than that! You must regard it as having been heard from the mouth of a prophet, and even beyond that, you must regard it as if you heard it from Moses himself . . . and even much more than that! You must regard it as if you have heard it from God himself."

—TALMUD

"What! *He* is now going to try to teach *me!*"—Why not? There is nobody from whom you cannot learn. Before God, who speaks through all men, you are always in the bottom class of nursery school.

—DAG HAMMARSKJÖLD

I say as Epicurus said, that a man should not so much respect what he eateth as with whom he eateth.

—MONTAIGNE

Rabbi Yohanan said: Had the Torah not been given us, we could have learned modesty from the cat, the command not to rob from the ant, chastity from the dove, and propriety from the cock.

—TALMUD

It is not thinking with the primitive ingenuity of childhood that is most difficult, but to think with tradition, with its acquired force and with all the accumulated wealth of its thought.

—AUGUSTE RODIN

Rabbi Nahman, son of Isaac, said:
Why are the words of the Torah compared to a tree,
as it is said: "She is a tree of life to them that lay hold upon
     her"? (Proverbs 3:18)
This is to tell you
that as a small log may set fire to a large log,
so do the lesser scholars sharpen the wits of the greater.
And Rabbi Hanina said the same:
Much have I learned from my masters,
and more from my comrades than from my masters,
and from my students the most.

—TALMUD

He who learns from his fellow a single chapter, a single rule, a single verse, a single expression, or even a single letter, ought to pay him honor.

—ETHICS OF THE FATHERS

The hints you have communicated from time to time not only deserve, but do most sincerely and cordially meet with my thanks. You cannot render a more acceptable service, nor in my estimation give a more convincing proof of your friendship, than by a free, open, and undisguised account of every matter relating to myself or conduct. The man who wishes to stand well in the opinion of others must do this; because he is thereby enabled to correct his faults, or remove prejudices which are imbibed against him. For this reason, I shall thank you for giving me the opinion of the world upon such points as you know me to be interested in; for, as I have but one capital object in view, I could wish to make my conduct coincide with the wishes of mankind, as far as I can consistently, I mean without departing from the great line of duty.

—GEORGE WASHINGTON

How can you expect to keep your powers of hearing when you never want to listen? That God should have time for you, you seem to take as much for granted as that you cannot have time for Him.

—DAG HAMMARSKJÖLD

"You can learn from everything," the rabbi of Sadagora once said to his hasidim. "Everything can teach us something, and not only everything God has created. What man has made has also something to teach us."

"What can we learn from a train?" one hasid asked dubiously.

"That because of one second one can miss everything."

"And from the telegraph?"

"That every word is counted and charged."

"And the telephone?"

"That what we say here is heard there."

—HASIDIC

Lastly come Experience, long conversant with the wise, the good, the learned, and the polite. Nor with them only, but with every kind of character, from the minister at his levee, to the bailiff in his spunging-house; from the dutchess at her drum, to the landlady behind her bar.

—HENRY FIELDING

Question: In the *Ethics of the Fathers* (4:1) we read: "Who is wise? He who learns from all men, as it is said, 'From all my teachers I have gotten understanding.'" (cf. Psalms 119:99) Then why does it not say: "He who learns from every teacher"?

Answer: The master who pronounced this dictum is intent on making it clear that we can learn not only from those whose occupation is to teach but from every man. Even from a person who is ignorant, or from one who is wicked, you can gain understanding as to how to conduct your life.

—HASIDIC

The unknown is the province of the student; it is the field for his life's adventure, and it is a wide field full of beckonings. Curiosity about it would drive a boy as well as a child to work through the known to get at the unknown.

—LINCOLN STEFFENS

. . . books are not absolutely dead things, but do contain a potency of life in them to be as active as that soul was whose progeny they are; nay, they do preserve as in a vial the purest efficacy and extraction of that living intellect that bred them. . . . Who kills a man kills a reasonable creature, God's image; but he who destroys a good book kills reason itself, kills the image of God, as it were in the eye.

—JOHN MILTON

The difference between a smart man and a wise one is this: A smart man can work his way out of a difficulty that a wise man will not get into in the first place.

—SAUL LIEBERMAN

The development of the intellect is the development of man.

—AUGUSTE COMTE

Said the Great Maggid to Rabbi Zusya, his disciple: "I cannot teach you the ten principles of service. But a little child and a thief can show you what they are.

"From the child you can learn three things:
He is merry for no particular reason;
Never for a moment is he idle;
When he needs something he demands it vigorously.

"The thief can instruct you in seven things:
He does his service by night;
If he does not finish what he has set out to do in one night, he devotes the next night to it;
He and those who work with him love one another;
He risks his life for slight gains;
What he takes has so little value for him that he gives it up for a very small coin;
He endures blows and hardship, and it matters nothing to him;
He likes his trade and would not exchange it for any other."

—HASIDIC

The more we understand individual things, the more we understand God.

—BARUCH SPINOZA

Familiarity with the great minds of the past and an acquaintanceship with many fields of knowledge yield versatility.

—ARTHUR G. COONS

Yosi, the son of Yoezer, of Zeredah, said: Let thy house be a meeting house for the wise, and sit in the very dust at their feet; and thirstily drink in their words.

—ETHICS OF THE FATHERS

Learning is never easy...

Words of Torah are compared with garments of delicate wool, which are not quickly acquired, but are speedily worn. So words of Torah are hard to acquire, but easy to lose. Words of foolishness, on the other hand, are like sackcloth, easy to buy, but not easy to tear. So words of folly are easy to acquire and hard to lose.

—FATHERS ACCORDING TO RABBI NATHAN

Of all the troubles, do not decline, as many people do, that of thinking.

—LORD CHESTERFIELD

We must try to help students see that there must be ideals and values and standards and consistency in applying them, but there must also be a flexible capacity to use them.

—ARTHUR G. COONS

Faith is a never-ending battle against self-absolutization and idolatry; it is a battle which has to be refought every moment of life because it is a battle in which the victory can never be final. But although never final, victory is always possible . . .

—WILL HERBERG

According to the effort, is the reward.

—ETHICS OF THE FATHERS

Truth springeth out of the earth;
And righteousness hath looked down from heaven.
Yea, the Lord will give that which is good;
And our land shall yield her produce.

—PSALMS 85:12–13

Raba observed: How dull-witted are those people who stand up before a Torah scroll and do not stand up before a great man!

—TALMUD

. . . Moses was good. He wanted to reveal more to the people, but he was not allowed. For it was God's will that the people make an effort of their own. Moses was to say just these words to them, no more and no less, so that they might feel: Something is hidden here, and we must strive to discover it for ourselves. That is why, further on, we read: "And he set before them all these words." (Exodus 19:7)

—HASIDIC

In the midst of the blare of commercial success we must recapture an honest respect for learning and for learned people. Abandoning that basic virtue in the first place was never meant to be a part of modern education and is part of no theory. It is one thing for us to glory in the tradition of the frontiersman in his buckskins who shouted "I'm as good as you are" to the whole world of bewigged and beribboned aristocracy, but it is quite another to allow a callow adolescent to slouch in his jeans and motorcycle jacket in smirking disrespect for a good and earnest physics teacher.

Democracy was never supposed to substitute license for discipline. Instead, it was meant to substitute self-discipline for oppression. But not even the most doctrinaire psychologists say that children can be expected to survive with self-discipline alone. Often they have to be told by both parents and teachers what to study and how to behave.

—SLOAN WILSON

There are seven marks of an uncultured, and seven of a wise man. The wise man does not speak before him who is greater than he in wisdom; and does not break in upon the speech of his fellow; he is not hasty to answer; he questions according to the subject matter, and answers to the point; he speaks upon the first things first, and the last last; regarding that which he has not understood he says, I do not understand it; and he acknowledges the truth. The reverse of all this is to be found in an uncultured man.

—ETHICS OF THE FATHERS

. . . the ultimate good desired is better reached by free trade in ideas—that the best test of truth is the power of the thought to get itself accepted in the competition of the market, and that truth is the only ground upon which their wishes can safely be carried out. That at any rate is the theory of our Constitution.

—OLIVER WENDELL HOLMES

If you take my advice, you will read the works I have listed, and then you will find that they suffice for everything you need to know. For it is not the quantity of what we read that counts, but its quality. Too much promiscuous reading may even harm beginners, just as too much food hurts children and invalids, and variety of presentation does not serve to increase the stores of the intellect. If merely a great number of books were the road to scholarship, the merchants who heap them up in towering piles would be the true sages. It is not enough to possess books; one must ponder their contents.

—JOSEPH SOLOMON DEL MEDIGO

He [Gaon of Vilna] is also reported to have said on one
occasion, he would not like to have an angel for his teacher
who would reveal to him all the mysteries of the Torah.
Such a condition is only befitting the world to come, but in
this world only things which are acquired by hard labor and
great struggle are of any value.

—SOLOMON SCHECHTER

Greater is learning [Torah] than priesthood and than royalty,
for royalty is acquired by thirty stages, priesthood by
twenty-four: but the Torah is acquired by forty-eight things
—by study, by diligent attention, by proper speech, by an
understanding heart, by a perceptive heart, by awe, by fear,
by humility, by joy, by attendance upon sages, by critical
give and take with fellows, by acute exchanges among disciples, by clear thinking, by study of Scripture, by study of
Mishna, by a minimum of sleep, by a minimum of chatter,
by a minimum pursuit of pleasure, by a minimum of frivolity,
by a minimum preoccupation with worldly matters, by long-
suffering, by generosity, by faith in the sages, by acceptance
of suffering.

—ETHICS OF THE FATHERS

I do not see how any man can afford, for the sake of his
nerves and his nap, to spare any action in which he can par-
take. It is pearls and rubies to his discourse. Drudgery,
calamity, exasperation, want, are instructors in eloquence and
wisdom.

—RALPH WALDO EMERSON

Besides being a thinker, man is a doer and an appreciator. I
doubt whether a college can give him much help as a doer.
Even as a thinker that is hard enough: "You can lead a girl
to Vassar, but you can't make her think."

—BRAND BLANSHARD

Faith consists in inmost conviction, not mere utterances . . .
faith is apprehension by the soul.

—MAIMONIDES

. . . knowledge of truth alone does not suffice; on the contrary this knowledge must continually be renewed by ceaseless effort, if it is not to be lost. It resembles a statue of marble which stands in the desert and is continuously threatened with burial by the shifting sand. The hands of service must ever be at work, in order that the marble continue lastingly to shine in the sun.

—ALBERT EINSTEIN

There is . . . creative reading as well as creative writing. When the mind is braced by labor and invention, the page of whatever book we read becomes luminous with manifold allusion.

—RALPH WALDO EMERSON

Where common sense proceeds in reckless haste, philosophy pauses and wonders. And were it merely a question of this gift, alone, this capacity to wonder, philosophy's rightful claim to superiority could not be disputed. For common sense, as it is said, is not addicted to the ways of wonder.

—FRANZ ROSENZWEIG

As wine, which though it have the taste of wine when new,
    the longer it ages in the cask, the better it tastes—
so with the words of Torah:
the longer they age in the body, the older they are, the better;
as it is said:
"Wisdom is with aged men, and understanding in length of
    days." (Job 12:12)
And as wine cannot keep either in a gold vessel or in a
    silver,
but in that which is the poorest of all vessels, an earthen
    vessel—
so the words of the Torah can keep only in one who makes
    himself humble.

—MIDRASH

To reduce poverty...

Genuine concern for the poor ...

The eight degrees of philanthropy, arranged according to their merit . . .

(1)—Helping the needy to be self-dependent by providing opportunity for work.

(2)—Giving charity to the poor in such a way that neither the donor nor the recipient knows one another.

(3)—Giving charity in such a way that the donor can identify the recipient but the recipient cannot identify the donor.

(4)—Giving in such a way that the recipient can identify the donor, but the donor cannot identify the recipient.

(5)—Giving in such a way that the donor and recipient know each other, providing the gift is made before it is requested.

(6)—Giving after a request is made, provided the amount is sufficient to meet the need.

(7)—Giving less than is needed, but with a kindly countenance.

(8)—Giving less than is needed, but without a kindly countenance.

—MAIMONIDES

We should never try to do anything for people unless we can do it with them, so as to preserve their dignity, their own sense of values, while contributing to a new prosperity.

—R. M. MACIVER

> Because I delivered the poor that
>   cried,
> The fatherless also, that had none
>   to help him.
> The blessing of him that was ready
>   to perish came upon me;
> And I caused the widow's heart to
>   sing for joy.
> I put on righteousness, and it
>   clothed itself with me;
> My justice was as a robe and a
>   diadem.
> I was eyes to the blind,
> And feet was I to the lame.
> I was a father to the needy;
> And the cause of him that I knew
>   not I searched out.

—JOB 29:12–16

From what source do some people derive their spontaneous intolerance of injustice, even though the injustice affects only others? And that sudden feeling of guilt at sitting down to a well-laden table, when others are having to go hungry?

—IGNAZIO SILONE

> Said Rabbi Judah, son of Rabbi Simon:
> The poor man sits and grumbles:
> "How am I different from that fellow?
>   Yet he sleeps in his bed, and I sleep here.
>   He sleeps in his house, and I here!"
> Now if you rise and give him something,
>   by your life,
> I shall consider it [says God]
>   as though you made peace between him and Me.

—MIDRASH

The coin which you drop into
The withered hand stretching toward
You is the only golden chain that
Binds your rich heart to the
Loving heart of God. . . .

—KAHLIL GIBRAN

"Deal thy bread to the hungry." When a person begs for food and clothing, there must be no investigation of his need, for we are told later: "When thou seest the naked . . . cover him." (Isaiah 58:7)

—TALMUD

. . . the shiftlessness, improvidence, and squalor, said to be characteristic of the poor, are the effect and not the cause of their poverty.

—PHILIP SOKOL

If all are the children of God, it follows that in their relation to one another they are brothers. And in this connection we note with interest, that, in most cases, when the Bible speaks of the poor man, or of one who was recently reduced to poverty, he is called "brother." "If thy brother be waxen poor, and sell some of his possession . . ."

—SOLOMON SCHECHTER

Once I resolved to devote a whole day to the recitation of the entire Book of Psalms. When towards evening I was approaching the end, the Sexton of my Rabbi came over to me, and said that the Rabbi wished to speak with me. I requested him to inform the Rabbi that I would see him as soon as I had finished.

But the Sexton returned and bade me come immediately. The Rabbi asked me: "Why did you not obey my first summons?" I explained the reason.

The Rabbi replied: "I called you to make a collection for a poor Jew. Psalms can be chanted by the Angels as well, but mortal men are needed to aid the destitute. Charity is a greater duty than the chanting of Psalms, inasmuch as the Angels cannot perform charity."

—HASIDIC

There is no quality and there is no power in man that was created to no purpose. And even base and corrupt qualities can be uplifted to serve God. When, for example, self-assurance is uplifted, it changes into proud assurance of the ways of God. But to what end can the denial of God have been created? It too can be uplifted through deeds of charity. For if someone comes to you and asks your help, you shall not turn him off with pious words, saying: "Have faith and take your troubles to God!" You shall act as though there were no God, as though there were only one person in all the world who could help this man—only yourself.

—HASIDIC

One's actions are a part of one's existence. . . . One feels it a duty to act, and whatever comes one does it—that's all—a very simple thing. I feel the capacity to *care* is the thing which gives life its deepest significance and meaning.

—PABLO CASALS

When Rabbi Levi Yitzhak accepted the call to become Rabbi of Berditchev, he stipulated that he should be invited to participate only in those meetings when new ordinances were to be decided. Once it was resolved to vote upon a prohibition against house-to-house begging by the poor. It was suggested that a public fund be substituted to aid them. The Rabbi was called, but he protested, saying: "Why do you summon me upon an old matter?" "But it is new," they said.

"You are mistaken," was his reply. "It is as old as Sodom and Gomorrah, where direct aid to the poor was forbidden. Perhaps they also had a public fund, the object of which was that the wealthy should be freed from the necessity of coming face to face with the poor."

—HASIDIC

Abba, son of Ba, gave Samuel his son money to divide
    among the poor.
He went out and found a poor man eating meat and drinking
    wine.
He came and told his father.
Abba said to him:
Give him more, for his soul is bitter.

—TALMUD

"Draw out thy soul to the hungry." (Isaiah 58:10)

If you really have nothing to give to a needy person, at least extend to him your words of comfort and encouragement by saying: "My soul goes out for you that I cannot help you." If you do at least this, your light will shine in the dark.

—MIDRASH

The poor we have ignored for so long will not move into suburbia tomorrow. But we must begin the long trek.

—EDWARD M. KEATING

There are four types of charity givers:

He who wishes to give but that others should not give— begrudges what belongs to others.

That others should give but not he—begrudges what belongs to himself.

That he should give and others too—the saint.

That neither he nor others give—the wicked.

—ETHICS OF THE FATHERS

If you don't really care, any reason is good enough.

—JOHN CIARDI

The generous [man] must take pains to spare, as much as possible, the feeling of the beneficiary of his generosity. "It is written," the rabbis remark, 'Happy is he who *considereth* the poor' (Psalms 41:2), and not 'Happy is he who *giveth* to the poor.'" Indeed great stress is laid on the manner in which we do our charity.

—SOLOMON SCHECHTER

Greater is the one who brings others to acts of charity than the one who does it himself.

—TALMUD

No one surrounded by
poverty can be rich…

Once some porters broke a barrel of wine belonging to
Rabbah, son of Rabbi Huna; so he took their clothing from
them. Thereupon they went to Rav, and he said to Rabbah:
"Give them back their clothing."

Rabbah replied: "Is this the law?"

Rav answered him: "Certainly! It is written: 'That thou
mayest walk in the way of good men.'" (Proverbs 2:20)

So he gave them back their clothing.

Hereupon they said to Rav: "We are poor and have toiled
all through the day; now we are hungry and we have
nothing."

Then Rav said to Rabbah: "Go and pay them their wages."

Rabbah replied: "Is this the law?"

Rav answered him: "Certainly! It is written: 'And keep the
paths of the righteous.'" (Proverbs 2:20)

—TALMUD

Here we are in the Atlantic world, 16 per cent of the world's peoples consuming 70 per cent of the world's wealth. We cannot be indifferent to the moral implications of this gap. I do not know how we can gain a new perspective about the narrow world of plenty and poverty in which we live unless moral insights of justice and compassion stir us to understand the privileged position in which we live.

—ADLAI E. STEVENSON

At the end of every three years, even in the same year, thou shalt bring forth all the tithe of thine increase, and shalt lay it up within thy gates. And the Levite, because he hath no portion nor inheritance with thee, and the stranger, and the fatherless, and the widow, that are within thy gates, shall come, and shall eat and be satisfied; that the Lord thy God may bless thee in all the work of thy hand which thou doest.

—DEUTERONOMY 14:28–29

. . . hungry, sick, and homeless people are a threat to world peace . . .

—JANE M. HOEY

. . . there must be a feeling of identification with the needy and underprivileged, a feeling that unless we make this a better world for them to live in, it cannot be the kind of world in which we can be contented. The fate of our dependent families is closely bound up with our own, and we can have no real salvation either in this world or the next, unless we can save the children of today from becoming the dependent families of tomorrow.

—PHILIP SOKOL

To every one who shows mercy to other men, mercy is shown from Heaven. But to him who shows no mercy to other men, no mercy is shown from Heaven.

—TALMUD

It is a basic assumption of democracy that there is a coincidence of the good of the individual with the good of society, that the pursuit of the good of the individual will in some way contribute to the quality, stability, and strength of the society.

—STERLING M. MCMURRIN

If a state is following System [the path], it is a disgrace to be in poverty and a low estate therein; if not, it is a disgrace to be rich and honored therein.

—CONFUCIUS

The wife of the Rabbi of Roptchitz said to him: "Your prayer was lengthy today. Have you succeeded in bringing it about that the rich should be more generous in their gifts to the poor?"

The Rabbi replied: "Half of my prayer I have accomplished. The poor are willing to accept them."

—HASIDIC

. . . now that technological advance has made the most distant peoples our neighbors, in such wise that our own fate is linked to theirs, now that our affluence includes the potential to inaugurate a situation in which all peoples can enjoy the minimum condition of a life no longer oppressed by sheer want and the ceaseless fear of want, charity in the old sense is outmoded and the call is for systems of economic equipment that in the mutual give-and-take of a world economic order will enable the hitherto helpless peoples to attain and maintain their own economic security.

—R. M. MACIVER

Thou shalt surely give him [the poor] and thy heart shall not be grieved when thou givest unto him; because that for this thing the Lord thy God will bless thee in all thy work; and in all that thou puttest thy hand unto.

—DEUTERONOMY 15:10

. . . the irresistible natural truth which we all abhor and repudiate: to wit, that the greatest of our evils, and the worst of our crimes is poverty, and that our first duty, to which every other consideration should be sacrificed, is not to be poor. "Poor but honest," "the respectable poor," and such phrases are as intolerable and as immoral as "drunken but amiable," "fraudulent but a good after-dinner speaker," "splendidly criminal," or the like. Security, the chief pretense of civilization, cannot exist where the worst of dangers, the danger of poverty, hangs over everyone's head . . .

—GEORGE BERNARD SHAW

. . . God is the real owner and proprietor of the land and all wealth found thereon. "The earth is the Lord's, and the fullness thereof," says the Psalmist. The same idea is conveyed to the rabbis by the declaration: "In the beginning God created the heaven and the earth." "Give unto Him of what is His, since thou and what thou hast are His." This is also found expressed by David who says: "For all things come of Thee and of Thine own have we given Thee." "If thou hast given charity, thou hast not given of thine own, but of His." "Thou shalt not say: 'I have no money' [to give to the poor], for all the money belongs to Him, as it is written: 'Mine is the silver and Mine is the gold saith the Lord of hosts.' " "Honor the Lord with thy substance," is emended by the rabbis so as to read: "Honor the Lord with what He has graciously given to thee." "Thou art My steward. If I gave thee aught, thou owest it to Me. Hence, give Me of My own."

—SOLOMON SCHECHTER

The ability to enjoy one's portion...

Ben Zoma says: . . . Who is a rich man? He that is content with his portion, as it is said: "When you eat the labor of your hands, happy shall you be, and it shall be well with you." (Psalms 128:2)

—ETHICS OF THE FATHERS

When a man partakes of his own, his mind is at rest; even if he partakes of what belongs to his father or mother or his children his mind is not at rest, and it is not necessary to add if he partakes of what belongs to strangers.

—FATHERS ACCORDING TO RABBI NATHAN

Had you better not stay at home, and live in peace and quietness, than go rambling up and down like a vagabond, and seeking for better bread than is made of wheat, without once so much as considering that many go to seek wool, and come home shorn themselves.

—MIGUEL DE CERVANTES

To have a liberal eye is to be content with one's portion and delight in what the Holy One, blessed be He, has given him.

If what he has is little, let him regard it as though it were plentiful. . . .

The opposite is true of the "grudging eye." If one acquires possessions and riches and honor, but regards it all as though it were only a little, and pursues the vanities of the world in order to satisfy his appetite for more and more, all his days are filled with pain, deep anguish, sickness and wrath.

—AKNIN

. . . one can overdo the business of complaining about the artificialities of our civilization. A symphony orchestra is as artificial as television. Penicillin is as artificial as neon lights. Most of the artificialities are designed to serve us in some important way. But the wise man turns his back on them occasionally and seeks to renew himself with the things he can see, hear and feel—direct contact with nature, face-to-face relations with his fellow man, fashioning something with his own hands.

—JOHN W. GARDNER

Rabbi Jonathan says: He who fulfills the Torah in poverty will in the end fulfill it in riches; but he who neglects the Torah in riches will in the end neglect it in poverty.

—ETHICS OF THE FATHERS

Two things have I asked of Thee;
Deny me them not before I die:
Remove far from me falsehood and lies;
Give me neither poverty nor riches;
Feed me with mine alloted bread;
Lest I be full, and deny, and say:
    "Who is the Lord?"
Or lest I be poor, and steal,
And profane the name of my God.

—PROVERBS 30:7-9

Rabbi Eliezer Ha-kappar says: Envy, lust, and hankering for glory put a man out of the world.

—ETHICS OF THE FATHERS

Great wealth, suddenly acquired, is not often enjoyed with
moderation, dignity and good sense.

—THOMAS BABINGTON MACAULAY

Rabbi Meir says:
Ever let a man teach his son a clean trade and an easy one,
and then let him pray to Him to Whom wealth and property
    belong.
For there is no trade which does not bring either poverty or
    wealth;
for the poverty does not come from the trade, and the wealth
    does not come from the trade, but all is according to a
    man's merit.

—MISHNAH

In our Transatlantick country we have a season, the calmest
and most delightful of the year, which we call the Indian
summer: I often say the autumn of our life resembles that
happy and serene weather: and am thankful for its rest and
its sweet sunshine.

—WILLIAM MAKEPEACE THACKERAY

He who forces time is forced back by time, but he who
yields to time finds time standing at his side.

—TALMUD

A man who is put to the trial . . . must give triple thanks to
the Almighty: first for giving him strength to endure the
trial, second for bringing the trial to an end, third for the
trial itself. For suffering contains the secret of creation and
its dimension of eternity; it can be pierced only from the
inside. Suffering betters some people and transfigures others.

—ELIE WIESEL

My poor friend, if you only knew that the Poverty
which causes you so much wretchedness is the
very thing that reveals the knowledge of
Justice and the understanding of Life, you
would be contented with your lot.

I say knowledge of Justice: for the rich
man is too busy amassing wealth to seek this
knowledge.

And I say understanding of Life: for the
strong man is too eager in his pursuit of
power and glory to keep to the straight
path of truth.

Rejoice then, my poor friend, for you are
the mouth of justice and the book of Life.
Be content, for you are the source of virtue
in those who rule over you and the pillar
of integrity of those who guide you.

—KAHLIL GIBRAN

Thus saith the Lord:
Let not the wise man glory in his
wisdom,
Neither let the mighty man glory
in his might,
Let not the rich man glory in his riches;
But let him that glorieth glory in
this,
That he understandeth, and knoweth
Me,
That I am the Lord who exercise
mercy,
Justice, and righteousness, in the
earth;
For in these things I delight,
Saith the Lord.

—JEREMIAH 9:22-23

The Rimanover Rabbi dreamed that he ascended to Heaven
and heard an angel pleading with the Lord to grant Israel
wealth, saying: "Behold how pious they are in poverty! Give
unto them riches and they will be many times as pious."

The Rabbi inquired the name of the angel. The reply was,
"He is called Satan."

The Rabbi then exclaimed: "Leave us in poverty, O Lord.
Safeguard us from the favors of Satan."

—HASIDIC

To reduce oppression...

Avoid gaining an advantage
at another's expense...

Question: Our sages say: "And there is not a thing that has not its place." (Ethics of the Fathers 4:3) And so man too has his place. Then why do people sometimes feel so crowded?
Answer: Because each wants to occupy the place of the other.

—HASIDIC

The cause of all these evils was the desire for power which greed and ambition inspire.

—THUCYDIDES

It has always been a mystery to me how men can feel themselves honored by the humiliation of their fellow-beings.

—MAHATMA GANDHI

Rabbi Joshua says: A grudging eye, evil impulse, and hatred of mankind put a man out of the world.

—ETHICS OF THE FATHERS

What is it to be a good citizen?

It is to acknowledge the other person's rights before asserting your own, but always to be conscious of your own.

It is to be free in word and deed, but it is also to know that your freedom is subject to the other person's freedom.

It is to create the useful and the beautiful with your own hands, and to admire what others have created in love and with faith.

—KAHLIL GIBRAN

Let a man forgive the disgrace to which he has been subjected.

Let him seek no honor through the disgrace of his neighbor.

—TALMUD

. . . Rabbi Israel Salanter found two boys quarreling over which was the taller. One forced the other to stand in a ditch to settle the argument. Seeing this, Rabbi Israel sadly commented, "Isn't this characteristic of the world where to prove his superiority man must prove others inferior? After all, the same purpose could have been achieved by standing on a chair!"

—LOUIS FINKELSTEIN

Rejoice not when your enemy falls, and let not your heart be glad when he stumbles. . . .

—PROVERBS 24:17

We ought . . . delicately and profoundly to respect one another's mental freedom; then only shall we bring about the intellectual republic; then only shall we have that spirit of inner tolerance without which all our outer tolerance is soulless . . . then only shall we live and let live, in speculative as well as practical things.

—WILLIAM JAMES

Say not unto thy neighbor: "Go, and come again,
And to-morrow I will give"; when thou hast it by thee.
Devise not evil against thy neighbor,
Seeing he dwelleth securely by thee.
Strive not with a man without cause,
If he have done thee no harm.

—PROVERBS 3:28–30

Who is a mighty man? He that subdues his evil impulse, as it
is said, "He that is slow to anger is better than the mighty,
and he that ruleth his spirit than him that taketh a city."
(Proverbs 16:32)

—ETHICS OF THE FATHERS

When you talk to people, do not weigh whether or not their
thoughts are clinging steadfastly to God. A soul that weighs
suffers harm.

—HASIDIC

It is a terrible, an inexorable, law that one cannot deny the
humanity of another without diminishing one's own: in the
face of one's victim, one sees oneself.

—JAMES BALDWIN

Rabbi Levi Yitzhak said: Whether a man really loves God—
that can be determined by the love he bears his fellow-men.
I shall give you a parable.

Once upon a time a country was suffering from the ravages
of war. The general who headed the army which was sent
against the foe was vanquished. The king discharged him
and put in his place another man who succeeded in driving
out the invader. The first general was suspected of betraying
his country. The king wondered whether there was any way
to find out whether he really loved or hated him. He realized
that there was one unerring sign which would discover the
truth to him: If the man, about whom he was in doubt,
showed friendship for the man who replaced him and ex-

pressed unalloyed joy at his success, he might be regarded as trustworthy; but if he plotted against his rival, this would prove his guilt.

God created man to strive against the evil in his soul. Now there is many a man who does, indeed, love God, but is defeated in that bitter struggle. He can be recognized by his ability to share whole-heartedly and without reservations in the happiness of his victorious fellow-man.

—HASIDIC

Keep strong, if possible. In any case, keep cool. Have unlimited patience. Never corner an opponent, and always assist him to save face. Put yourself in his shoes—so as to see things through his eyes. Avoid self-righteousness like the devil—nothing is so self-blinding.

—B. H. LIDDELL HART

When the rich man tells the poor man: "Why don't you go to work? Look how well you are built, how strong you are, what fine muscles you have."

God retorts: "It is not enough that you don't give him anything; you even begrudge him what I gave him."

—MIDRASH

"Whenever you feel like criticizing anyone . . . just remember that all the people in this world haven't had the advantages that you've had."

—F. SCOTT FITZGERALD

Enrich your heart with love and friendship, so that you love your neighbor as yourself; wish him well, have mercy upon him in his misfortune, and do not observe his fall with malicious pleasure, but grieve in your heart for the sad fate that has struck him who is like you. Make all effort in his behalf, so that you may live to see him re-established, rejoice in his solace, and boast of his friendship.

—JACOB BEN WOLF KRANZ

The humble man uplifts
all around him...

Rabbi Joseph said:
Ever let a man learn from the wise ways of his Creator.
For lo, the Holy One, blessed be He, ignored all the high
    mountains and hills, and settled His Presence on Mount
    Sinai,
and ignored all the goodly trees, and settled His Presence on
    the thornbush.

—TALMUD

We live in an era whose humblest men are becoming greater
than the greatest men of preceding ages.

—KAHLIL GIBRAN

Rabbi Moshe Leib of Sassov once gave his last coin to a man
of evil reputation. His students reproached him for it. Where-
upon he replied: "Shall I be more particular than God, who
gave the coin to me?"

—HASIDIC

Better it is to be of a lowly spirit with the humble,
Than to divide the spoil with the proud.

—PROVERBS 16:19

Be wiser than other people if you can, but do not tell them
so.

—LORD CHESTERFIELD

I will tell you, scholar, I have heard a grave divine say that
God has two dwellings, one in heaven and the other in a
meek and thankful heart.

—IZAAK WALTON

There are some dispositions in regard to which it is wrong
to pursue a middle course, but the contrary extreme is to be
embraced, as for instance in respect to pride. One does not
follow the proper path by merely being humble. Men should
be very humble and extremely meek. To this end Scripture
says of Moses our Teacher that he was "very meek" (Numbers 12:3) . . . therefore the command of the Sages is, "Be
thou very humble . . ."

—MAIMONIDES

Everyone who humbles himself, God exalts; and everyone
who exalts himself, God humbles; one who runs around for
greatness, greatness flees from him; and one who flees from
greatness, him greatness pursues.

—TALMUD

Rabbi Simeon . . . expounded: Always be as supple as the
reed, not rigid as a cedar. A reed, even though the four
winds of the world ride forth, the reed bends with them and
straightens with them; when the winds are still, the reed
again stands in its place. And the end of this reed? It is considered worthy for the making of the pen that writes the
scroll of the Torah.

But not so with the cedar: if a wind blows from the north-
west, it tears it down, if it blows from the southwest, it blows

it down and hurls it upon its face. And thus it is found: cast down is the cedar that stood so high upon its roots. And the end of this cedar? Loggers come and chop it up and use it to build houses, and what is left they throw into the fire.

This is why the sages said: Be supple as a reed; do not be rigid as a cedar.

—TALMUD

There is something in our life which is nobler and more supreme than fame; and this *something* is the great deed that invokes fame.

—KAHLIL GIBRAN

. . . knowledge of what *is* does not open the door directly to what *should be*. One can have the clearest and most complete knowledge of what *is* and yet not be able to deduct from that what should be the *goal* of our human aspirations.

. . . mere thinking cannot give us a sense of the ultimate and fundamental ends. To make clear these fundamental ends and valuations, and to set them fast in the emotional life of the individual, seems to me precisely the most important function which religion has to perform in the social life of man.

—ALBERT EINSTEIN

Rabbi Ishmael taught: When a man travels the right path in life, everyone looks to him with awe and respect. When he sins, he is afraid of everyone.

—MIDRASH

It is an absolute perfection, and as it were divine for a man to know how to enjoy his being loyally. We seeke for other conditions because we understand not the use of ours, and goe out of our selves forsomuch as we know not what abiding there is. It is vain to get upon stilts, for be we upon them, yet must we goe with our owne legges. And sit we upon the highest throne of the World, yet sit we upon our owne taile. The best and most commendable lives and best pleasing men are (in my conceit) those which are fitted to the common mould and human model, without wonder or extravagancy.

—MONTAIGNE

Rabbi Pinhas, son of Yair, said: The Torah leads to deliberation, deliberation leads to zeal, zeal leads to cleanness, cleanness leads to continence, continence leads to purity, purity leads to godliness, godliness leads to humility, humility leads to saintliness, saintliness leads to [possession of] the holy spirit, the holy spirit leads to eternal life; but among all the qualities, saintliness is the greatest—As it is written: "Thou spokest in vision to Thy saintly ones." (Psalms 89:20)

Rabbi Joshua, son of Levi, objected to this, for Rabbi Joshua, son of Levi, said: Humility is the greatest among them all—As it is written: "The spirit of the Lord God is upon me; because the Lord hath anointed me to bring good tidings unto the humble." (Isaiah 61:1)

—TALMUD

The ideal is ultimately best
(most practical) for all...

Said Rabbi Bunam: "The verse 'Justice, justice shalt thou pursue' (Deuteronomy 16:20) teaches us that we may use only justifiable methods even in the pursuit of justice."

—HASIDIC

Is not love known to be better than hatred and charity better than revenge, are not hypocrisy and cowardice by everyone condemned, and is not civilization based on truth-telling, which might be called a physical fact inasmuch as we have a machine that detects a lie? . . . Who fails to respond to the theme of *The Glass Menagerie* of Tennessee Williams that "purity of heart is the one success worth having"?—as most of us share Voltaire's respect for tolerance and good temper . . . So how, in the face of this general agreement, can one doubt the existence of values? And how can one doubt that these values are deeply rooted in the general mind, for all its indiscipline, grossness and worship of success?

—VAN WYCK BROOKS

We live in an age when ultimate questions have, quite unaccountably, become immediate questions.

—WILL HERBERG

[175]

. . . if man is to prevail, reason must also prevail. This is not to be Utopian . . . but to be coldly realistic.

—EDWARD M. KEATING

He that oppresseth the poor blasphemeth his Maker;
But he that is gracious unto the needy honoreth Him.

—PROVERBS 14:31

"Man's right to knowledge and the free use thereof" is more than a noble phrase. It supplies an approach to domestic and international affairs that is at once both hard-headed and idealistic. Its basic theme is the equality of men; for man's right to knowledge and the free use thereof includes every man, whatever his race, creed, or color. Recognition of this principle of equality is the key to most of the political and social problems that beset this troubled world.

—WILLIAM O. DOUGLAS

And his delight shall be in the fear of the Lord;
And he shall not judge after the sight of his eyes,
Neither decide after the hearing of his ears;
But with righteousness shall he judge the poor,
And decide with equity for the meek of the land;
And he shall smite the land with the rod of his mouth,
And with the breath of his lips shall he slay the wicked.

—ISAIAH 11:3–4

Never be mean in anything; never be false; never be cruel. Avoid those three vices, Trot, and I can always be hopeful of you.

—CHARLES DICKENS

Better is a little with righteousness
Than great revenues with injustice.

—PROVERBS 16:8

Culture will always be in peril where criticism cannot be freely practiced.

—ANDRÉ GIDE

> The liberty of discussion is the chief safeguard of all other liberties.
>
> —THOMAS BABINGTON MACAULAY

And when ye reap the harvest of your land, thou shalt not wholly reap the corner of thy field, neither shalt thou gather the gleaning of thy harvest. And thou shalt not glean thy vineyard, neither shalt thou gather the fallen fruit of thy vineyard; thou shalt leave them for the poor and for the stranger: I am the Lord your God. Ye shall not steal; neither shall ye deal falsely, nor lie one to another. And ye shall not swear by My name falsely, so that thou profane the name of thy God: I am the Lord. Thou shalt not oppress thy neighbor, nor rob him; the wages of a hired servant shall not abide with thee all night until the morning. Thou shalt not curse the deaf, nor put a stumbling-block before the blind, but thou shalt fear thy God: I am the Lord. Ye shall do no unrighteousness in judgment; thou shalt not respect the person of the poor, nor favor the person of the mighty; but in righteousness shalt thou judge thy neighbor. Thou shalt not go up and down as a talebearer among thy people; neither shalt thou stand idly by the blood of thy neighbor: I am the Lord. Thou shalt not hate thy brother in thy heart; thou shalt surely rebuke thy neighbor, and not bear sin because of him. Thou shalt not take vengeance, nor bear any grudge against the children of thy people, but thou shalt love thy neighbor as thyself: I am the Lord.

—LEVITICUS 19:9–18

> When we are unhurried and wise, we perceive that only great and worthy things have any permanent and absolute existence, that petty fears and petty pleasure are but the shadow of the reality. This is always exhilarating and sublime.
>
> —HENRY DAVID THOREAU

Let a man keep himself pure of pernicious gossiping, for thus spoke our masters, blessed be their memory: Whosoever recounts pernicious gossip is like one who denies the divine principle, for it is written: "Who have said: 'Our tongue will we make mighty; our lips are with us: who is lord over us?' " (Psalms 12:5) And likewise is a man forbidden to listen to pernicious gossip.

Thus spoke our masters, blessed be their memory: Four groups cannot receive the Divine Presence, and these are the group of those who scoff, the group of those who lie, the group of those who flatter, and the group of those who recount pernicious gossip.

And let a man keep himself pure from bearing tales, as it is written: "Thou shalt not go up and down as a talebearer among thy people." (Leviticus 19:6)

—RABBI JONAH

So long as ignorance and misery remain upon the earth, so long will books of this kind be demanded . . . Destroy the cave, Ignorance, and you destroy the mole, Crime . . .

—VICTOR HUGO

The real slavery of Israel in Egypt was that they had learned to endure it.

—HASIDIC

Good is that which makes for unity;
Evil is that which makes for separateness.

—ALDOUS HUXLEY

If we believe in nothing, if nothing has any meaning and if we can affirm no values whatsoever, then everything is possible and nothing has any importance. . . . Evil and virtue are mere chance or caprice.

—ALBERT CAMUS

. . . the task of education is really very intricate and involved, and it moves with reference to the most intangible, hidden elements of the mind. We cannot be more practical than to strive to build the mental and moral capacity of our young people.

—ARTHUR G. COONS

. . . ethics have a practical value, inseparable from their ultimate one: the creation of better men and women. Rivalry for goodness should, in the long run, make for pragmatic gain.

—LOUIS FINKELSTEIN

Extending the good from generation to generation...

A traveler once saw an old man planting a carob tree. "When will the tree bear fruit?" asked the traveler. "Oh, perhaps in seventy years," the old man answered.

"Do you expect to live to eat the fruit of that tree?" "No," said the old man, "but I didn't find the world desolate when I entered it, and as my fathers planted for me before I was born, so do I plant for those who come after me."

—TALMUD

. . . I want somebody on that hilltop or its equivalent who can be thinking and looking far ahead and who can prod me into doing the things that it would be easier not to do. Don't try to think of things that are politically shrewd. . . . Try to think of the next generation.

—ADLAI E. STEVENSON

Question: In the Book of Elijah we read: "Everyone in Israel is duty-bound to say: 'When will my works approach the works of my fathers, Abraham, Isaac and Jacob?'" How are we to understand this? How could we ever venture to think that we could do what our fathers did?

Answer: Just as our fathers invented new ways of serving, each a new service according to his own character: one, the service of love; another, of stern justice; a third, of beauty; so each one of us in his own way should devise something new in the light of the teaching and of service, and do what has not yet been done.

—HASIDIC

The first Duke of Marlborough, asked by a snob, "Whose descendant are you?" replied, "I am not a descendant. I am an ancestor."

—ANONYMOUS

Religion, occupying herself with personal destinies and keeping thus in contact with the only absolute realities which we know, must necessarily play an eternal part in human history.

—WILLIAM JAMES

You have all been taught by Lord Macaulay and his school that because you have Carpets instead of rushes for your feet; and Feather-beds instead of fern for your backs; and Kickshaws instead of beef for your eating; and Drains instead of Holy Wells for your drinking;—that, therefore, you are the Cream of Creation, and every one of you a seven-headed Solomon. Stay in those pleasant circumstances and convictions if you please; but don't accuse your roughly bred and fed fathers of telling lies about the aspect the earth and sky bore to *them*,—till you have trodden the earth as they, barefoot, and seen the heavens as they, face to face.

—JOHN RUSKIN

Do not exalt the leaders of former generations in order to undermine the authority of leaders of your day: "Jephthah in his generation may be as valuable as Moses in his day."

—TALMUD

It seems a clever and a daring feat to set up models of our own; but it is in reality much easier than toiling after the old unapproachable models of our forefathers. The originality which dispenses so blithely with the past is powerless to give us a correct estimate of anything that we enjoy in the present.

—AGNES REPPLIER

This is the true greatness, which descended direct from Adam. He was the noblest creature on earth. Therefore you rank above all the other inhabitants of the earth.

—JUDAH HA-LEVI

During the last century in the Western World, the aggrandizement of the machine and the degradation of man went hand in hand. Yet the moral energies which had accumulated in Western Europe in the course of twenty-five hundred years or more did not immediately die out.

—LEWIS MUMFORD

The historic fact is that art is shy, and seldom comes at all; and when it does come it is founded on folklore, tradition, and a reverence for the past.

—JOHN JAY CHAPMAN

. . . historians ought to be precise, faithful, and unprejudiced, and neither interest nor fear, hatred nor affection, should make them swerve from the way of truth, whose mother is history, the rival of time, the depositary of great actions, the witness of the past, example to the present, and monitor to the future.

—MIGUEL DE CERVANTES

Rabbi Simeon, son of Eleazar, says: Greater is he who acts righteously out of love, than one who acts from fear. Good action from fear has an influence for a thousand generations, but righteous acts out of love influence two thousand generations.

—TALMUD

I am convinced that what the nation needs desperately is a renewed sense of Western tradition, really a sense that we are involved in a living, evolving civilization. We need an awareness of continuity with the past, an abiding affirmation of the humanistic and philosophic values learned so painfully through the long centuries of our common experience.

—JOHN COGLEY

You must demonstrate that you are worthy of your heroic past.

—S. M. DUBNOW

As no air pump can by any means make a perfect vacuum, so neither can any artist entirely exclude the conventional, the local, the perishable from his book, or write a book of pure thought, that shall be as efficient, in all respects, to a remote posterity as to contemporaries, or rather to the second age. Each age, it is found, must write its own books; or rather, each generation for the next succeeding.

—RALPH WALDO EMERSON

Think not in your heart that the Torah is an inheritance from your fathers, and needs no personal effort to win it. The matter is not so. If you toil not therein, you shall not acquire, and more than ordinary will be your punishment; in that you forsake your family tradition. So we read in tractate [of Talmud] Nedarim: "Why do not learned fathers invariably beget learned children? Rabbi Joseph answered: 'So that people shall not say your Torah is inherited from your fathers.' "

—HEBREW ETHICAL WILLS

5. THE THREE LEVELS OF SOLVING PROBLEMS

The Three Levels of Solving Problems
. . . in Ourselves, Our Family, Our Work, Our City, Our
Nation, Our World.

What happens when we are sick?
We turn to a doctor to cure what is wrong: to stop an
infection or to repair an injury. It's the most familiar way
to treat an illness—*after* it has occurred.

This is the *curative* level.

There is another level of medicine. We now use vaccines
to prevent polio; and science continues to find new ways
to protect us from disease after disease.

This is the *preventive* level.

There remains a third level in the care of our bodies.
Medical science seeks not only to cure and prevent illness
but also to perfect our health; to bring new strength and
zest into our daily life through fullness of health.

This is the *perfective* level.

And wherever we turn, we find the same three levels of
meeting any problem.

In Our Family
What can we do when communication breaks down with
those closest to us—when we talk at cross-purposes, or re-
treat into silence, with members of our own family?

At the curative level

Someone must take the first step to reestablish communication, saying in effect: "Let us try again. Let the past be past. We can start anew."

At the preventive level

We try to listen more patiently. We do not build up walls within our family with harsh or unfeeling words. We discipline our ways of speech—and so keep communication flowing.

At the perfective level

We understand and enjoy those near to us for what they are—and can become. We then spontaneously find many things to do together, and to talk about. These, in turn, *enlarge* our family life, generating still more love and sharing within the home.

In Our Work

What if we are frustrated or bored in our work?

At the curative level

What has gone wrong may be in us or in the job. We may be in the wrong place or even the wrong career. What is then required to fulfill our talents is the courage to change our place or our field of work.

At the preventive level

Our work may be necessary yet not absorbing; nor may it be practical for us to change. But many wonderful people manage to achieve full lives, despite the commonplace demands of their daily tasks. For there are always meaningful opportunities for each of us to develop rich values and new interests *outside* our work.

At the perfective level

We find more in our work than just "making a living." Each day we open doors to something new and better: in what we do, in our fellow-workers, and in ourselves—exploring the endless paths of creativity *wherever we are.*

In Our City

When violence makes us fear to walk on our streets and in our parks, what can we do?

At the curative level

Provide more policemen to guard our streets and parks.

At the preventive level

Be concerned, not only with the *wrong*, but with the *wrongdoer*, seeking to help, not merely to punish.
Guide undirected young energies toward new horizons they cannot find alone.

At the perfective level

With our steadily increasing skills and resources, we can build a *great* city . . . where *all* our young can grow up in decent dwellings, schools and neighborhoods—so that young and old develop inner resources to enrich the community instead of attacking it.

In Our Nation

Democracy is an unfinished business in our land.

At the curative level
Pass laws to eliminate legal injustice and economic hopelessness, wherever these may remain in the United States.

At the preventive level
Recognize fully the interdependence of all groups in our society and all parts of our nation; realizing that no one can be sure of his freedom, or of his livelihood, when others are restricted in theirs.

At the perfective level
Advance from *adequacy* to *excellence* in American life; setting still higher standards of achievement for ourselves, and in service to mankind.

In Our World
The nations of the world continue to fear each other.

At the curative level
Deter force by force—in competing blocs of nations which divide the world.

At the preventive level
Create an enduring world order through world law, maintaining peace through a world police.

At the perfective level
With the peoples of the world now living within sight and sound of each other, *live as neighbors, everywhere*

on earth—working to increase together all that is good for the Family of Man.

Whoever we are—whether we find the problem in ourselves, in our family, in our work, in our city, in our nation, or in our world—what we *do* about our problems is ultimately determined by our character.

And each of us has been given the power:
to shape his character,
to train himself in good action,
to choose between right and wrong,
to raise himself and those around him to better levels of life,
practicing the wisdom of Micah:

"To do justice, to love mercy, and to walk humbly before your Lord." (Micah 6:8) ·

The curative level
of solving problems...

Avoiding errors...

If anyone has committed a serious sin, let him beware of thinking of it. For where our thoughts are, there we also are with our soul. Let not our soul sink into the mire of sin; it may not be able to extricate itself and repent.

And even if a man has committed a minor offense, why should he think of it? Why should he· place his soul in the mire? Turn mire hither and thither, and it remains mire. What good can come to Heaven from disturbing your sin in your mind? During the time thus consumed you may perform a good deed which will truly be like presenting God with a pearl.

Turn away from evil; hold it not in remembrance; do good. If you have sinned much, balance it by doing much good. Resolve today, from the depth of your heart and in a joyful mood, to abstain from sin and to do good.

—HASIDIC

Men who have once engaged in a wicked and perilous enterprise are no longer their own masters, and are often impelled, by a fatality which is part of their just punishment, to crimes such as they would at first have shuddered to contemplate.

—THOMAS BABINGTON MACAULAY

What can one say about Chelm? It was a town like all the other towns in the old country. It was little. But it had a big problem.

The only road to Chelm was steep and narrow and full of curves. People were always falling off and getting hurt. That was the problem.

When the Fishman fell over the cliff and couldn't deliver the fish for Friday, the situation began to look serious. When the Mailman lost some very important letters, things looked even worse. But when the Milkman couldn't deliver milk for the newborn babies, the wise men of Chelm decided that something had to be done.

So they held a meeting. They discussed. They debated. Six days and six nights they deliberated, and at the last minute before the Sabbath, they reached a decision. And what did they decide?

They built a hospital at the bottom of the cliff.

—FOLK TALE

Failure to repent is much worse than sin. A man may have sinned for but a moment, but he may fail to repent of it moments without number.

—HASIDIC

It is written: "Take heed unto yourselves, lest ye forget the covenant of the Lord your God, which He made with you, and make you a graven image, even the likeness of anything which the Lord thy God hath bidden thee" (Deuteronomy 4:23), and not—as the meaning really demands—"which the Lord thy God hath forbidden thee."

"The Torah warns us," said the zaddik who had been listening, "not to make a graven image of anything the Lord our God has bidden us."

—HASIDIC

This suspicion against overzeal, which might make it possible for man not to be on the Lord's side even when in the service of a righteous cause, is one against which man has constantly to be on his guard . . .

Zeal and enthusiasm are only of value when they are balanced by experience and sound judgment, only to be acquired by mature age and after many a bitter disappointment.

—SOLOMON SCHECHTER

Procrastination is the thief of time—collar him.

—EDWARD YOUNG

A man is endowed by nature with two eyes; one to see his neighbor's virtues, and the other to view his own failings.

—HASIDIC

For roughness; it is a needless cause of discontent: severity breedeth fear, but roughness breedeth hate. Even reproofs from authority ought to be grave, and not taunting.

—FRANCIS BACON

Depart from evil, and do good; seek peace and pursue it.

—PSALMS 34:15

A man has not every thing to do, but something; and because he cannot do *every thing*, it is not necessary that he should do *something* wrong.

—HENRY DAVID THOREAU

Slander slays three persons; the speaker, the listener, and the one who is being slandered.

—TALMUD

The circumstances of the times in which we have happened to live, and the particular period, placed us in a state of apparent opposition, which some might suppose to be personal also; and there might not be wanting those who wished to make it so, by filling our ears with malignant falsehoods. . . . And if there had been at any time, a moment when we were off our guard, and in a temper let the whispers of these people make us forget what we had known of each other for so many years, and years of so much trial, yet all men . . . who have seen the false colors under which passion sometimes dresses the actions and motives of others, have seen also those passions subsiding with time and reflection, dissipating like mists before the rising sun, and restoring us the sight of all things in their true shape and colors. It would be strange indeed, if, at our years, we were to go back an age to hunt up imaginary or forgotten facts, to disturb the repose of affections so sweetening to the evening of our lives. Be assured, my dear sir, that I am incapable of receiving the slightest impression from the effort now made to plant thorn on the pillow of age, worth and wisdom, and to sow tares between friends who have been such for nearly half a century. Beseeching you, then, not to suffer your mind to be disquieted by this wicked attempt to poison its peace, and praying you to throw it by among the things which have never happened, I add sincere assurances of my unabated and constant attachment, friendship and respect.

—THOMAS JEFFERSON

Whoever runs after greatness, greatness flees from him; and whoever flees from greatness, greatness runs after him. "Then why," a disciple asked his Rabbi, "has greatness been avoiding me? I have really been fleeing from it." "The trouble is," the Rabbi answered, "when you run away from it you keep turning your head to see if greatness is following you."

—HASIDIC

All genuine ideals have one thing in common: they express the desire for something which is not yet accomplished but which is desirable for the purposes of the growth and happiness of the individual. We may not always know what serves this end, we may disagree about the function of this or that ideal in terms of human development, but this is no reason for a relativism which says that we cannot know what furthers life or what blocks it. We are not always sure which food is healthy and which is not, yet we do not conclude that we have no way whatsoever of recognizing poison. In the same way we can know, if we want to, what is poisonous for mental life.

—ERICH FROMM

Lord, who shall sojourn in Thy tabernacle? . . .
He that walketh uprightly, and worketh righteousness,
And speaketh truth in his heart;
That hath no slander upon his tongue,
Nor doeth evil to his fellow . . .

—PSALMS 15:1–3

It is the usual result of a sudden and unexpected gleam of prosperity on a people that it makes them vainglorious and arrogant. Good fortune attained as a consequence of judicious measures is more likely to last than what bursts upon us at once. And, to conclude, men are much more dexterous in warding off adversity than in preserving prosperity.

—THUCYDIDES

We poor mortals have to be on our guard not to know too much, and be satisfied with guesses and hypotheses. All that we can aspire to are mere glimpses.

—SOLOMON SCHECHTER

In giants we must kill pride and arrogance: but our greatest foes, and whom we must chiefly combat, are within. Envy we must overcome by generosity and nobleness of soul; anger, by a reposed and easy mind; riot and drowsiness, by temperance and vigilance . . .

—MIGUEL DE CERVANTES

If we could hang all our sorrows on pegs and were allowed to choose those we liked best, everyone of us would take back his own, for all the rest would seem even more difficult to bear.

—HASIDIC

Doing the minimum...

Rabbi Tarfon used to say: It is not your duty to finish the work, but neither are you at liberty to neglect it.

—ETHICS OF THE FATHERS

Man is born, not to solve the problems of the universe, but to find out where the problem applies, and then to restrain himself within the limits of the comprehensible.

—JOHANN WOLFGANG VON GOETHE

. . . When I was a youth, newly married, I lived with my father-in-law, a watchmaker. I desired greatly to visit a famous Rabbi, but had no money for the journey. I said to my father-in-law:

"If you will give me a few dollars, I will repair the little watch with which you have had no patience to bother." He agreed, and I took apart the watch to discover the cause of the difficulty. I soon saw that nothing was lacking, but that a tiny hairspring was twisted. This I soon made straight, placed everything together and the watch began to keep time once more.

Does this not teach that a slight twist of the heart often halts the normal moral feeling? A little adjustment and the heart beats properly again.

—HASIDIC

Few are qualified to shine in company; but it is in most
men's power to be agreeable.

—JONATHAN SWIFT

. . . it matters not how small the beginning may seem to be:
what is once well done is done for ever.

—HENRY DAVID THOREAU

Worry about your own soul and the next person's body—and
not the opposite.

—HASIDIC

Before God confers greatness on a man, He first tests him
by a little thing and then promotes him to greatness.

Witness two great leaders whom God first proved by a little
thing, found trustworthy and then promoted to greatness.

He tested David with sheep, and David led them only
through the wilderness, in order to keep them from despoiling private fields. God said to him, "You have been found
trustworthy with the sheep, come therefore and tend My
sheep."

Similarly, in the case of Moses, "he led the flock to the
farthest end of the wilderness" (Exodus 3:1) in order to keep
them from despoiling private fields. God therefore took him
to tend Israel.

—MIDRASH

. . . moral virtue comes about as a result of habit, whence
also its name *ethike* is one that is formed by a slight variation
from the word *ethos* (habit).

—ARISTOTLE

Rabbah, son of Rabbi Huna, taught: He who has knowledge
of the Law, but no fear of God, is like a keeper of a treasury
who has the inner keys but not the outer keys. How is he
to enter?

—TALMUD

Selection begins with refusal.

—JOHN CIARDI

Conduct, as Matthew Arnold put it, is three-fourths of life; and to have no theory of conduct, to have no discipline of conduct, to be unaware that there is a deliberate art of conduct, is to leave the personality itself in a raw, uncultivated state.

—LEWIS MUMFORD

Men are foolish enough in their desire for vengeance to make precedent against themselves by infringing those laws which are the common protection of mankind and from which alone they can expect aid if they fall into difficulties.

—THUCYDIDES

Let every man make known what kind of government would command his respect, and that will be one step toward obtaining it.

—HENRY DAVID THOREAU

. . . the purpose of law, either for man or his group, is to create those conditions that inhibit the negative tendencies and favor the positive ones. This is done by defining obligations, setting up deterrents to antisocial or criminal behavior, and dealing with violations.

—NORMAN COUSINS

He who tries to do more than he is able, will in the end do less . . .

—AKNIN

The more faithfully you listen to the voice within you, the better you will hear what is sounding outside. And only he who listens can speak. Is this the starting point of the road toward the union of your two dreams—to be allowed in clarity of mind to mirror life and in purity of heart to mold it?

—DAG HAMMARSKJÖLD

I am more carefull to encrease my health when it smiles upon me, then to recover it when I have lost it.

—MONTAIGNE

The Rabbi of Berditchev saw a man hurrying along the street, looking neither right nor left. "Why are you rushing so?" he asked him. "I am after my livelihood," the man replied. "And how do you know," continued the Rabbi, "that your livelihood is running on before you, so that you have to rush after it? Perhaps it is behind you, and all you need do to encounter it is to stand still—but you are running away from it!"

—HASIDIC

Courage to act...

Every man is created twice: Once when he is born; second when he repents and takes on new courage to live in ways more acceptable to God.

—HASIDIC

Shall we strike sail, avoid a certain experience so soon as it seems not expressly calculated to increase our enjoyment or our self-esteem? Shall we go away whenever life looks like turning in the slightest uncanny, or not quite normal, or even rather painful and mortifying? No, surely not. Rather stay and look matters in the face, brave them out; perhaps precisely in so doing lies a lesson for us to learn.

—THOMAS MANN

There is resiliency in the soul of man and he may lie down to bleed awhile and return refreshed.

—HEYWOOD CAMPBELL BROUN

No man lives by denying life.

—ANDRÉ MALRAUX

Man must recognize that it is not easy to repent and turn away from his customary bad habits. One must battle and conquer the inclination which diverts a person from the good path. There is a great reward for the one who masters the impulse to do wrong. . . . Succeeding in this task is like the struggle of a sick person who, in order to cure his illness, must resist certain foods and tempting delicacies and take bitter and unpleasant medicine. So too, a repentant person must discipline himself and resist temptation. It is wise to emphasize the other extreme of one's passion and thus strive hard to resist the attractive but harmful deed—just as a sick person must withstand the attractions of certain food. For actually evil behavior is the greatest malady and only one who turns away from it is really healthy, as it is written, "Return ye backsliding children; I will heal your backslidings" (Jeremiah 3:22), and it is written, "Who [God] forgiveth all thine iniquity; who healeth all diseases." (Psalms 103:3)

—MENORAT HAMAOR

Life yields only to the conqueror. Never accept what can be gained by giving in. You will be living off stolen goods, and your muscles will atrophy.

—DAG HAMMARSKJÖLD

Not everything that is faced can be changed; but nothing can be changed until it is faced.

—JAMES BALDWIN

Don't be disgusted, don't give up, don't be impatient if you do not carry out entirely conduct based in every detail upon right principles; but after a fall return again, and rejoice if most of your actions are worthier of human character. Love that to which you go back . . .

—MARCUS AURELIUS

Rabbi Isaac said:
If a man says to you, I have toiled and I have not found
—do not believe him.
I have not toiled and I have found
—do not believe him.
I have toiled and I have found
—believe him.

—TALMUD

When the morning's freshness has been replaced by the weariness of midday, when the leg muscles quiver under the strain, the climb seems endless, and, suddenly, nothing will go quite as you wish—it is then that you must *not* hesitate.

—DAG HAMMARSKJOLD

The Tzupenester Rabbi found his disciples playing checkers. He said: "You may learn much wisdom from the rules of this game. You surrender one in order to capture two. You may not make two moves at one time. You must move up and not down. When you reach the top, you may move as you like."

—HASIDIC

If thou faint in the day of
adversity,
Thy strength is small indeed.

—PROVERBS 24:10

Worry has been defined as the act of borrowing trouble from the future for present-day consumption; and courage has been defined as the act of borrowing hope from the future for present-day consumption. . . . One of the by-products of religious faith is the hopeful outlook described by Isaiah: "The mind stayed on Thee, Thou keepest in perfect peace because it trusteth in Thee." (Isaiah 26:3)

—MAX ARZT

The brave man carves out his fortune, and every man is the son of his own works.

—MIGUEL DE CERVANTES

When people are merry and dance, it sometimes happens that they catch hold of someone who is sitting outside and grieving, pull him into the round, and make him rejoice with them. The same happens in the heart of one who rejoices: grief and sorrow draw away from him, but it is a special virtue to pursue them with courage and to draw grief into gladness, so that all the strength of sorrow may be transformed into joy.

—HASIDIC

Constancy of character is tested whenever a crisis occurs and a decision is called for. We readily sustain our principles when no sacrifice is entailed. But too often we rationalize their abandonment when the situation calls for heroic disregard of immediate personal comfort or interest.

—MAX ARZT

. . . man can be as big as he wants. No problem of human destiny is beyond human beings.

—JOHN F. KENNEDY

The Holy One, blessed be He, the Lord, who is called righteous and upright, has not created man "in His own image" save in the sense that man be as righteous and upright as He Himself.

Perhaps you will ask why the Holy One, blessed be He, has created the evil urge, of which it is written: "for the imagination of man's heart is evil from his youth." The Holy One Himself says that it is evil; who then could render it good?

The Holy One, blessed be He, replies: You yourself are he who makes it evil. How? A child of five, or six, of seven, eight, or nine years does not sin. Not until he is ten years old does he begin to sin; it is then he raises the evil urge, so that it grows big.

Perhaps you will say: Man cannot help himself! The Holy One, blessed be He, answers: There are so many things in the world that are mightier than the evil urge and more bitter, and yet thou make them sweet. You will find nothing more bitter than the lupine, but you take the trouble to boil it in water seven times over, and to sweeten it until it grows sweet; and so it is with mustard, and capers, and many other things. If you sweeten then for your use the bitter things I have created, how much more you could do with the evil urge, which was given into your hand.

—MIDRASH

The preventive level of solving problems...

Do not demand the impossible of yourself... or others...

Man is like a tree. If you stand in front of a tree and watch it incessantly, to see how it grows, and to see how much it has grown, you will see nothing at all. But tend it at all times, prune the runners and keep it free of beetles and worms and—all in good time—it will come into its growth. It is the same with man: all that is necessary is for him to overcome his obstacles, and he will thrive and grow. But it is not right to examine him hour after hour to see how much has already been added to his stature.

—HASIDIC

The Rabbis ask why God began the Ten Commandments with the Hebrew word "anochi." After all, there is a simpler Hebrew word for "I," namely "ani."

To this they respond: "The word for 'I' in Egyptian is 'anuch.' When the Jews came out of Egypt, they knew very little Hebrew but knew Egyptian. Thus the Almighty opened the Ten Commandments with the Egyptian word, so that the people would understand. By starting on the level of their understanding, it was possible to bring to them the next Hebrew word of the Ten Commandments, namely, 'The Lord.' "

—MIDRASH

Do what you can—and the task will rest lightly in your hand, so lightly that you will be able to look forward to the more difficult tests which may be awaiting you.

—DAG HAMMARSKJÖLD

All beginnings are difficult.

—MIDRASH

We are not so foolish as to believe you can overturn everything that has taken centuries to develop. But we insist that the first steps be taken.

—EDWARD M. KEATING

A king asked his son to hire two men to fill a deep pit.

The first, a stupid worker, upon looking into the pit, exclaimed in despair, "How can I fill so deep a cavern?" The other, a wise worker, said, "What concern is it of mine that the pit is so deep? I am hired by the day and I shall therefore perform my day's work."

So God says to us: "What concern is it of yours that the Torah is so extensive and that there is so much to learn? You are hired to do My work from day to day. All that I expect of you is to perform a full day's work in the study of Torah."

—MIDRASH

He hath past his life in idleness, say we; alas! I have done nothing this day. What? have you not lived? It is not onely the fundamentale but the noblest of your occupation. Had I beene placed or thought fit for the managing of great affaires, I would have showed what I could have performed. Have you knowne how to meditate and manage your life? you have accomplished the greatest work of all. . . . Have you knowne how to compose your conduct? you have done more than he who hath composed bookes. Have you knowne how to take rest? you have done more than he who hath taken Empires and Citties. The glorious masterpiece of man is to live properly. . . .

—MONTAIGNE

When you accuse a sinner and pronounce judgment upon
him, saying that he deserves such and such a misfortune, you
are pronouncing judgment upon yourself. Though the tres-
pass of the other may be alien to your soul, you must have
trespassed in some such way yourself. If you accuse him of
idol worship, for example, you have probably been guilty
of pride, and that is just as if you yourself had served an
idol. And your guilt may be even greater. For you are subject
to sterner judgment. But if you justify the sinner and point
to the fact that he is still prisoned in his flesh and cannot
govern his urges, then you are justifying yourself.

—HASIDIC

> There are few things *wholly* evil, or *wholly* good. Almost
> every thing . . . is an inseparable compound of the two; so
> that our best judgment of the preponderance between them
> is continually demanded.
>
> —ABRAHAM LINCOLN

> "And make a fence for Torah." (Ethics of the Fathers 1:1)
> A vineyard with a fence is better than one without it.
> But a man should not make a fence higher than the object
> which it is to guard, lest the fence fall and crush the plants.
> This is what Adam did; he had a fence higher than the
> object, and the fence fell and crushed the plants.
>
> —FATHERS ACCORDING TO RABBI NATHAN

To rejoice at a success is not the same thing as taking credit
for it. To deny oneself the first is to become a hypocrite
and a denier of life; to permit oneself the second is a childish
indulgence which will prevent one from ever growing up.

—DAG HAMMARSKJÖLD

> Always, when I see something badly done or not done at all,
> I see an opportunity to make a fortune. I never kick at bad
> work by my class: there's lots of it and we suffer from it.
> But our failures and neglects are chances for the young fel-
> lows coming along and looking for work.
>
> —RUDOLPH SPRECKELS

Justice must be tempered with mercy.

At first God created the world strictly on the principle of justice. Seeing, however, that the world could not endure on that basis alone, He added thereto the principle of mercy, so that when man sinned, justice, which would demand his immediate punishment, might be tempered with mercy.

—MIDRASH

Be concerned to help
the wrongdoer...

. . . as I live, saith the Lord God, I have no pleasure in the
death of the wicked, but that the wicked turn from his way
and live . . .

—EZEKIEL 33:11

"You shall go in His ways." (Deuteronomy 28:9) What are
His ways? Just as it is God's way to be merciful and forgiving to sinners and to receive them in their repentance, so
do you be merciful to one another. Just as God is gracious
and gives gifts gratis both to those who know Him and to
those who know Him not, so do you give gifts [freely] one
to another.

Just as God is long-suffering to sinners, so be you long-
suffering to one another.

—MIDRASH

. . . The truly devout are easily recognized . . . their piety
is human, is reasonable. They do not condemn all our actions.
They think there is too much arrogance in these censures.
Leaving haughty words to others, they reprove our actions
by their own. They do not build upon the appearances of
evil, and their minds are inclined to think well of others. No

spirit of cabal is in them, and they have no intrigues to scent out; their sole care is to live rightly. They do not persecute a sinner; it is only the sin itself they hate. Nor do they desire to vindicate the interests of Heaven with a keener zeal than Heaven itself shows. These are the people I admire; that is the right way to live.

—MOLIÈRE

If it happens to anyone that he sees something sinful or hears of it, he should know that in himself there is a small particle of this sin, and let him make it his business to set it right.

—HASIDIC

There were some lawless men living in the neighborhood of Rabbi Meir and they used to vex him sorely. Once Rabbi Meir prayed that they should die.

His wife, Beruriah, exclaimed, "What is in your mind? Is it because it is written: 'Let sinners cease out of the earth'? (Psalms 104:35) But the text can read so as to mean, 'Let *sins* cease out of the earth.' Glance at the end of the verse, 'and let the wicked be no more,' that is, when 'sins shall cease' then 'the wicked will be no more.' Rather should you pray that they repent and be no more wicked." Rabbi Meir offered prayer on their behalf and they repented.

—TALMUD

I must forgive the lovelessness, the hatred, the slander, the fraud, the arrogance which I encounter, since I myself have so often lacked love, hated, slandered, defrauded, and been arrogant. I must forgive without noise or fuss. In general I do not even get as far as being merely just.

—ALBERT SCHWEITZER

As in the case of the hoe with which one digs in filth, and to which filth always clings, so it is with him who reproves without being perfect in righteousness himself.

—HASIDIC

. . . he who desires to assist other people, either by advice or by deed . . . will avoid referring to the vices of men, and will take care only sparingly to speak of human impotence, while he will talk largely of human virtue or power and of the way by which it may be made perfect, so that men, being moved not by fear or aversion but solely by the emotion of joy, may endeavor as much as they can to live under the rule of reason.

—BARUCH SPINOZA

A hasid complained to Rabbi Wolf that certain persons were turning their nights into days, playing cards. "That is good," said the zaddik. "Like all men, they too wish to serve God, and do not know how. But now they are learning to stay awake and to persevere in doing something. When they have become perfect in this, all they have to do is to turn to God —and oh, what servants they will then make for God!"

—HASIDIC

Every man beareth the whole stampe of humane condition.

—MONTAIGNE

Salty and wind-swept, but warm and glittering. Keeping in step with the measure under the fixed stars of the task. How many personal failures are due to a lack of faith in this harmony between human beings, at once strict and gentle.

—DAG HAMMARSKJÖLD

You do not destroy an idea by killing people; you replace it with a better one.

—EDWARD M. KEATING

When the Egyptians were drowning in the sea, the angels wanted to sing songs of exaltation. But the Holy One, blessed be He, disapproved, saying: "The work of my hands are drowning in the sea, and you are singing!"

—TALMUD

The perfective level
of solving problems...

Appreciate what you are...
and can become...

No limits are set to the ascent of man, and the loftiest precincts are open to all. In this, your choice alone is supreme.

—HASIDIC

God that gives the wound may give the remedy. This is one day, but tomorrow is another . . .

—MIGUEL DE CERVANTES

Betake yourself to the gardens of good ways, slowly and patiently, according to what your condition makes possible.

And be forewarned of excess that knows not step by step, and of distractions, so that you may not lose yourself; for if there is too much oil in the lamp, the light will go out.

And be forewarned as well of evasion, of indolence, and of slackness. Rather, let zeal follow upon zeal, step for step, let suffering be followed by new suffering, add to every step of the good way that which is above it, and do not evade examining your heart, but think of it constantly with your soul.

—BAHYA IBN PAKUDA

"Ye are My witnesses, saith the Lord, and I am God." (Isaiah 43:12) When you are my witnesses [in your good acts], I am God, and when you are not my witnesses, I am not God.

—MIDRASH

As the births of living creatures at first are ill-shapen, so are all innovations, which are the births of time.

It were good, therefore, that men, in their innovations, would follow the example of time itself, which indeed innovateth greatly, but quietly, and by degrees scarce to be perceived.

—FRANCIS BACON

Going up a mountain path one day, I met a mountaineer with an ax in his hand. I walked with him and asked him what he was going to cut. "I need a piece of timber to fix my wagon," he said. "I need the toughest kind of wood I can get. That kind always grows on top of the mountains where all the storms hit the hardest."

We are prone to lament that the world is not better. Yet the fact that it is full of trouble affords us our only chance to spend our hearts. A time of prosperity is a dangerous time; the soul loafs and grows fat. Times of storm and peril are the ones to show what we are made of. A storm is always a challenge; there seems to be something in the heart that rises up to meet it.

—ARCHIBALD RUTLEDGE

Idealism must always prevail on the frontier, for the frontier, whether geographical or intellectual, offers little hope to those who see things as they are. To venture into the wilderness, one must see it, not as it is, but as it will be. The frontier, being the possession of those only who see its future, is the promised land which cannot be entered save by those who have faith.

—CARL BECKER

Rabbi Levi said: There are six things which serve man; three are in his control, and three are not. Eye, nose and ear are not. He must see, smell and hear what he may not want to see, smell and hear. A man may be passing through a street when incense is being burnt to an idol, and he has no wish to smell the incense, but his nose forces him to do so. So, too, his eye brings him sinful sights, and his ear blasphemous words, against his will, for they too are not under his control.

But mouth, hand and foot are in his power. He need not desire with his mouth to labor in the law. He need not wish with his hand to fulfill the commandments. He need not wish to steal or murder. With his foot he can visit the theatre or circus, or he can go to the synagogue or house of study.

—MIDRASH

Let us endeavor so to live that when we come to die even the undertaker will be sorry.

—MARK TWAIN

Besides being civil, which is absolutely necessary, the perfection of good breeding is to be civil with ease.

—LORD CHESTERFIELD

Everything is foreseen [by God], yet freedom of choice is granted [to man]; the world is judged in mercy, and all depends on the preponderance of [good or ill] doing.

—ETHICS OF THE FATHERS

They say that characters were engraven on the bathing tub of King Tching-thang to this effect: "Renew thyself completely each day; do it again, and again, and forever again." . . . After a partial cessation of his sensuous life, the soul of man, or its organs rather, are reinvigorated each day, and his Genius tries again what noble life it can make.

—HENRY DAVID THOREAU

He bore failure without self-pity and success without self-admiration.

—DAG HAMMARSKJÖLD

Happiness settles the spirit, but sorrow drives it into exile.

—HASIDIC

All men want, not something to *do with*, but something to *do*, or rather something to *be*.

—HENRY DAVID THOREAU

Achievement is not a station in life, it is a way of traveling.

—ANONYMOUS

I knew a man that had health and riches, and several houses, all beautiful, and ready-furnished, and would often trouble himself and family to be removing from one house to another; and being asked by a friend why he removed so often from one house to another, replied, "It was to find content in some one of them." But his friend, knowing his temper, told him, if he would find content in any of his houses, he must leave himself behind him; for content will never dwell but in a meek and quiet soul.

—IZAAK WALTON

The reason Americans have not trapped the bluebird of happiness . . . is that happiness as total gratification is not a state to which man can aspire.

—JOHN W. GARDNER

Of all the intellectual achievements . . . the one, I think, that is most truly civilized is that by and large we have learned to deal with man as he is and not as we suppose he ought to be.

—J. WILLIAM FULBRIGHT

Intelligence recognizes what has happened. Genius recognizes what will happen.

—JOHN CIARDI

A man is known by three names. The first is the name which his parents give him; the second is the name by which others call him; and the third is the name by which he is identified in the true record of his life, from birth to death.

—MIDRASH

Seek the creative opportunity
in the everyday...

Soon after the death of Rabbi Moshe, Rabbi Mendel of Kotzk asked one of his disciples: "What was most important to your teacher?" The disciple thought and then replied: "Whatever he happened to be doing at the moment."

—HASIDIC

I know of no more encouraging fact than the unquestionable ability of man to elevate his life by a conscious endeavor. It is something to be able to paint a particular picture, or to carve a statue, and so to make a few objects beautiful; but it is far more glorious to carve and paint the very atmosphere and medium through which we look, which morally we can do. To affect the quality of the day, that is the highest of arts. Every man is tasked to make his life, even in its details, worthy of the contemplation of his most elevated and critical hour. . . . Simplicity, simplicity, simplicity! I say, let your affairs be as two or three, and not a hundred or a thousand; instead of a million count half a dozen, and keep your accounts on your thumbnail.

—HENRY DAVID THOREAU

Human felicity is produced, not so much by great pieces of good fortune that seldom happen, as by little advantages that occur every day.

—BENJAMIN FRANKLIN

I embrace the common; I explore and sit at the feet of the familiar, the low. Give me insight into today, and you may have the antique and future worlds. . . . Man is surprised to find that things near are not less beautiful and wondrous than things remote. The near explains the far.

—RALPH WALDO EMERSON

Unless we believe that God renews the work of creation every day, our prayers and obeying of the commandments grow old and accustomed, and tedious. As it is written in the psalm: "Cast me not off in the time of old age" (Psalms 71:9) . . . that is to say, do not let my world grow old.

And in Lamentations it is written: "They are new every morning: great is Thy faithfulness." (Lamentations 3:23) That the world is new to us every morning—that is Your great faithfulness!

—HASIDIC

I have no special revelation of God's will . . . He reveals Himself daily to every human being, but we shut our ears to the "still small voice."

—MAHATMA GANDHI

Rabbi Eliezer said: "Turn to God the day before you die." And his disciples asked him: "Does a man know on which day he will die?"

And he answered them, saying: "Just because of this, let him turn to God on this very day, for perhaps he must die on the morrow, and thus it will come about that all his days will be the days of turning to God."

—TALMUD

When I hear people say they have not found the world and life so agreeable or interesting as to be in love with it, or that they look with equanimity to its end, I am apt to think they have never been properly alive nor seen with clear vision the world they think so meanly of, or anything in it—not a blade of grass.

—W. H. HUDSON

Love is always the first time again. Whatever comes after
that is only habituation.

—JOHN CIARDI

Is not this quality of joy the most precious fruit of the civilization which is ours? A totalitarian tyranny, too, might
satisfy us in our material needs. But we are not beasts to be
fattened. Prosperity and comfort could never of themselves
wholly satisfy our needs. For us, brought up to believe in
human respect, simple meetings which sometimes change into
wonderful occasions are heavy with meaning.

—ANTOINE DE SAINT-EXUPÉRY

God says to man as He said to Moses: "Put off thy shoes
from off thy feet"—put off the habitual which encloses your
foot and you will recognize that the place on which you
happen to be standing at this moment is holy ground. For
there is no rung of being on which we cannot find the holiness of God everywhere and at all times.

—HASIDIC

An American soldier in France won the Croix de Guerre
but refused to wear it, and this is his explanation: "I was
no good back home. I let my sister and my widowed mother
support me. I was a dead beat. And now they have given
me the Croix de Guerre for something I did at the front.
I am not going to put it on. I am going back home first. I am
going to win out there. I am going to show my mother that
I can make good at home. Then I will put on the Croix de
Guerre." He is not the only one who has discovered that
being heroic in a crisis is sometimes easier than being useful
at home.

—HARRY EMERSON FOSDICK

Boredom is what happens when we lose contact with the
universe. Nor does it matter whether or not the universe
is in contact with us. It exists as whatever it is, and we exist
only as we react to it.

—JOHN CIARDI

The newspaper has discovered that most people most of the time are interested in some form of catastrophe: a plane crash, a railroad wreck, a murder, a flood, a scandal, a fight of some sort. It is an old story that the planes that fly safely, the trains that reach their destination, the individuals who live together without murdering each other, the rivers that flow between their banks, and the men and nations that transact their affairs and resolve their differences without fighting are not news. Not one of these would yank a man out of his own preoccupations as he passed a newsstand.

—H. A. OVERSTREET

To gaine a Battaile, perfourme an Ambassage, and governe a people, are noble and woorthy actions; to chide, laugh, sell, pay, love, hate, and mildely and justly to converse both with his owne and with himselfe; not to relent, and not gaine-say himselfe, are thinges more rare, more difficult . . .

—MONTAIGNE

Happy is the generation where the great listen to the small, for it follows in such a generation the small will listen to the great.

—TALMUD

She would rather light candles than curse the darkness . . .

—ADLAI E. STEVENSON

The day will happen whether or not you get up.

—JOHN CIARDI

God makes every occupation pleasant to those who follow it.

—TALMUD

Establish the highest
goal–excellence...

It is written, "Mingled with oil." (Numbers 15:4) This is the Law, which must be mingled with good works, as it is taught, "Splendid is the study of the Law, when combined with a worldly occupation." (Ethics of the Fathers 2:2) Man gives pleasure to his Maker when he busies himself with the study of the Law, does good deeds, and refrains from sin.

—MIDRASH

Whatever is worth doing at all is worth doing well.
—LORD CHESTERFIELD

We want meaning in our lives. When we raise our sights, strive for excellence and dedicate ourselves to the highest goals of our society, we are enrolling in an ancient and meaningful cause: the age-long struggle of man to realize the best that is in him.

—JOHN W. GARDNER

The realization of great ideas, heaven-conceived and earth-born, is not accomplished without travail and woe, deep sorrow and repeated disappointment.

—SOLOMON SCHECHTER

God keep me from ever completing anything. This whole book is but a draught—nay, but the draught of a draught. Oh, Time, Strength, Cash, and Patience!

—HERMAN MELVILLE

Do not pray for easy lives. Pray to be stronger men! Do not pray for tasks equal to your powers. Pray for powers equal to your tasks.

—PHILLIPS BROOKS

Never look down to test the ground before taking your next step: only he who keeps his eye fixed on the far horizon will find his right road.

—DAG HAMMARSKJÖLD

Rabbi Mendel of Kotzk said: "And these words which I command thee this day, shall be *upon* thy heart." (Deuteronomy 6:6) The verse does not say *"in* thy heart." For there are times when the heart is shut. But the words lie upon the heart, and when the heart is open in holy hours, they sink deep down into it.

—HASIDIC

The performance of a boat pilot who guided a large ocean liner into port was praised by a viewer: "You certainly know where all the shallow places are and avoid them so well." Answer: "You are wrong on that. I know where the deep waters are to be found."

—ANONYMOUS

In the ebb and flow of a period of rapid change in the world, it is well to remember that there are all kinds of individuals and little groups of people who find security in abiding spiritual values, and with complete dedication seek to find ways of preserving them. During the invasion of southern Europe by "the barbarians," copies of the original text of the Scriptures were hidden in various places so that they might not be destroyed. People in secret caves, in forests, and wherever they could find hiding places, kept alive the spirit of devotion to the needs of suffering humanity.

—CLARENCE E. PICKETT

Micah came and comprised them [the 613 commandments of the Torah] in three. For it is written:
"It hath been told thee, O man, what is good, and what the Lord doth require of thee:
Only to do justly, and to love mercy, and to walk humbly with thy God."
And again it was Isaiah who comprised them in two. As it is written:
"Thus saith the Lord: Keep ye justice, and do righteousness.
And Amos came and comprised them in one, as it is said: "For thus saith the Lord unto the house of Israel: Seek ye Me, and live."
To this Rabbi Nahman, son of Isaac, objected and said: That would mean, "Seek Me" in observing the entire Torah "and live"! But it is Habakkuk who came and comprised them in one. As it is written: "But the righteous shall live by his faith."

—TALMUD

Honesty is the ability to resist small temptations. Saintliness is the ability to resist large ones—or is it the inability to recognize them?

—JOHN CIARDI

It is written: "Pure olive oil beaten for the light." (Exodus 27:20) We shall be beaten and bruised, but in order to glow —not to grovel!

—HASIDIC

I feast, I cherish and I embrace truth, where and in whom soever I finde it, and willingly and merily yeeld my selfe unto her, as soone as I see but her approach, though it be a farre-off, I lay downe my weapon and yeeld my selfe vanquished.

—MONTAIGNE

Rabbi Yohanan said to them [his five disciples]: Go forth and see which is the right way to which a man should cleave.

Rabbi Eliezer replied: A liberal eye.
Rabbi Joshua replied: A good companion.
Rabbi Yosi replied: A good neighbor.
Rabbi Simeon replied: Foresight.
Rabbi Elazar replied: A good heart.

Thereupon Rabbi Yohanan, the son of Zakkai, said to them: I prefer the answer of Elazar, for in his words your words are included.

—ETHICS OF THE FATHERS

"No one," Cyrus always said, "can be a good officer who does not undergo more than those he commands."

—XENOPHON

. . . however powerful and responsive economic and political instruments may be, they are not enough in themselves to produce a good society and good lives for its members. These instruments will produce what is good, desirable, and valuable only if the people want what is good, desirable, and valuable.

—COMMITTEE FOR ECONOMIC DEVELOPMENT

The strong personality, the well-formed character, results not only from being able surely to follow through logical thought in some process of reasoning, but also in being able to relate that thinking and reasoning to action.

—ARTHUR G. COONS

. . . thoroughness is a part of excellence, and . . . self-complacency is the companion of ignorance.

—SOLOMON SCHECHTER

There are times when I feel like a boy. As long as you are able to admire and to love, you are young. And there is so much to admire and to love. . . . Look at the sea, the sky, trees, flowers! A single tree—what a miracle it is! What a fantastic, wonderful creation this world is, with such diversity. That is the law of nature—diversity.

—PABLO CASALS

. . . I dread success. To have succeeded is to have finished one's business on earth, like the male spider, who is killed by the female the moment he has succeeded in his courtship. I like a state of continual *becoming*, with a goal in front and not behind.

—GEORGE BERNARD SHAW

6. IF NOT NOW...WHEN?

"IF NOT NOW . . . WHEN?"

In the lifetime of your children?
In your lifetime?
This year?
This day?

Look at Your Hand . . .

You can move it!
. . . as a caress or a fist; to build up or tear down, to give
or to take.

Always, your hand can make a mistake or correct one.
Or it can do nothing.

So with your heart and your mind, as with your hand.
They can serve your need alone . . . or serve another . . .
or serve no one.

The decision is yours.

This is the wonder, and the challenge, of our lives.

For the harsh fact of our lives is how free we are to do
nothing. Or to do the wrong thing: to hurt not only
others but ourselves.

Yet the great thing of our lives is how free we are *to start
again;* to find a better path—from whatever wrong turn
we or our world may have taken.

We are not caught forever in any error or confusion.

The power is ours to move again.

"IF NOT NOW . . . WHEN?"

Look at Yourself . . .

For whom has the power to move been given, if not for
you, so that you can be responsible for meeting your
own needs?

You have every right—indeed the obligation—to do so:
—the right to use your heart, your mind and your hand, to advance your standard of living; to enjoy the blessing which today's world makes possible.
—the right to seek and earn the respect of those around you; to achieve recognition of your talents and your efforts.

And who but *you* should strive for a better life for your family, a promising future for your children?

"IF I AM NOT FOR MYSELF, WHO WILL BE?"

Look at Your Neighbor . . .

Aren't his children as dear to him as yours are to you?

Isn't his self-respect as necessary to his as yours is to you?

And if *he* is denied the freedom and opportunity to serve his own needs, to fulfill his obligations, to enjoy his rights, what happens to you?

For you are your neighbor's neighbor.

And it is only together that you can possibly achieve the kind of community you want for yourself, for your own family and for the family of man.

"IF I AM FOR MYSELF ALONE, WHAT AM I?"

Look at the World . . .

Even as we can reach out our hand to give or to take, to build or to tear down, so men everywhere can now easily move their ideas, their values and themselves, to *any* corner of the earth—to give or to take, to build or to tear down.

Whether as an individual, a family, a community or a nation, we are no longer alone.

We all live in one place.

Thus, there is no longer any such thing as poverty "there." It is poverty "here."

There is no such thing as ignorance "there." It is ignorance "here."

There is no such thing as oppression "there." It is oppression "here."

Again, this is the wonder and the challenge of our lives.

As we seek wisdom and freedom and sustenance for ourselves, *we can only hope to reach and maintain these goals as we are concerned that others achieve them too . . . creating them together.*

For . . . "If I am not for myself, who will be?

    If I am for myself alone, what am I?

    If not now, when?" (Ethics of the Fathers 1:14)

If I am not for myself, who will be...?

Each person is unique...

In every man there is something precious, which is in no
one else. And so we should honor each for what is hidden
within him, for what only he has, and none of his comrades.

—HASIDIC

The fundamental law of nature is not equality but variety. . . .
This variety, which is the basis and stepping stone of the
harmony of the Cosmos, is the result of the process of dif-
ferentiation, which becomes more and more accentuated, the
higher we rise in the scale of nature, and reaches its culmina-
tion in man and human aggregates. Every form of existence
in nature, be it an object, a man, or a nation, has its own
distinct place in the Universe, which can truly be filled only
by itself—and by no other.

—ISRAEL FRIEDLAENDER

Even a single grain of wheat is not exactly like another.

—TALMUD

. . . I pity those who . . . despise others because they're not
the same as themselves. . . .

—MARK VAN DOREN

My soul is my counsel and has taught me to give ear to the voices which are created neither by tongues nor uttered by throats.

—KAHLIL GIBRAN

Every person born into this world represents something new, something that never existed before, something original and unique. ". . . there has never been anyone like him in the world, for if there had been someone like him, there would have been no need for him to be in the world. Every single man is a new thing in the world and is called upon to fulfill his particularity in this world."

—MARTIN BUBER

Joy is the effect which comes when we use our powers. Joy, rather than happiness, is the goal of life, for joy is the emotion which accompanies our fulfilling our natures as human beings. It is based on the experience of one's identity as a being of worth and dignity . . .

—ROLLO MAY

We haven't the time to be ourselves. All we have time for is happiness.

—ALBERT CAMUS

"And He [God] said, I am the God of your father." (Exodus 3:6) The Holy One, Blessed be He, revealed Himself to him [Moses] in the voice of his father Amram, so that he should not be frightened. For one should address the ear [of a person] according to his capacity. At that moment Moses rejoiced, saying, my father is still alive. [Then] God said to him: "I am the god of your father, the God of Abraham . . . (Exodus 3:6), I approached you subtly so as not to frighten you. Immediately Moses hid his face . . ." (Exodus 3:6)

From this the sages taught: Happy is he who recognizes his own place and stands in his own place.

—MIDRASH

Our composition, both public and private, is full of imperfection; yet is there nothing in nature unserviceable, no not inutility it selfe; nothing thereof hath beene insinuated in this huge universe but holdeth some fit place therein.

—MONTAIGNE

One young man of my acquaintance, who has inherited some acres, told me that he thought he should live as I did, *if he had the means*. I would not have anyone adopt *my* mode of living on any account; for, beside that before he has fairly learned it, I may have found out another for myself, I desire that there may be as many different persons in the world as possible . . .

—HENRY DAVID THOREAU

One may acquire eternity in a single moment [by the change in a person with one great action].

—TALMUD

Another sign of our times, also marked by an analogous political movement, is the new importance given to the single person. Everything that tends to insulate the individual—to surround him with barriers of natural respect, so that each man shall feel the world is his, and man shall treat with man as a sovereign state with a sovereign state—tends to true union as well as greatness.

—RALPH WALDO EMERSON

The great failure of education—not just in the United States but throughout most of the world—is that it has made man group-conscious rather than species-conscious. It has celebrated man's institutions but not man himself. It has attached value to the things man does but not to what man is. Man's power is heralded but the preciousness of life is unsung.

. . . There are national anthems but no anthems for humanity.

—NORMAN COUSINS

If you see a crowd of human beings, say: "Blessed art Thou our Lord, King of the Universe, Who knowest the secret minds of man."

As the faces of men are unlike one another, so their dispositions are unlike one another; each one has his own disposition.

So when Moses was about to die, he besought God and said: "Known and revealed to Thee is the disposition of all men, and the dispositions of Thy children are unlike one another. When I am removed from them, I beseech You to appoint over them a leader who may bear with each one according to his disposition."

—MIDRASH

One must be true to oneself...

Rabbi Zusya said, a short while before his death: "In the world to come I shall not be asked: 'Why were you not Moses?' I shall be asked: 'Why were you not Zusya?'"

—HASIDIC

. . . Whenever I have been afraid that my work was so personal that no one could understand it, everybody did understand it. When I tried to speak for others, they didn't know what I was talking about.

—MARK VAN DOREN

When a man leaves his own rung and takes that of his friend, he will not be fruitful on either the one rung or the other. Many followed the example of Rabbi Simeon, son of Yohai, and their work did not succeed because they were not of his quality, but only did as he did, in imitation of his quality.

—HASIDIC

If man is to have confidence in values, he must know himself and the capacity of his nature for goodness and productiveness.

—ERICH FROMM

If a man intended to perform a good deed and was prevented, he is regarded as though he had actually carried it out.

—TALMUD

Never, "for the sake of peace and quiet," deny your own experience or convictions.

—DAG HAMMARSKJÖLD

It is impossible to tell men what way they should take. For one way to serve God is by the teachings, another by prayer. another way by fasting, and still another by eating. Everyone should carefully observe which way his heart draws him, and then choose that way with all his strength.

—HASIDIC

If any organism fails to fulfill its potentialities, it becomes sick, just as your legs would wither if you never walked. But the power of your legs is not all you would lose. The flowing of your blood, your heart action, your whole organism would be weaker. And in the same way if man does not fulfill his potentialities as a person, he becomes to that extent constricted and ill.

—ROLLO MAY

"The soul that does not know God is a leaf detached from the tree, a single, solitary leaf, that falls to the ground, dries up, and rots. But the soul that is given to God is like a leaf attached to the tree. By means of the vital sap that nourishes it, it communicates with the branches, the trunk, the roots, and the whole earth."

—IGNAZIO SILONE

He who takes gestures, idioms, etiquette for the human being will not get to know the human being.

—KARL JASPERS

We are soon known by those around us for who we *are*
rather than what we would like others to think about us.
This is a man's "character" in the profoundest sense of the
word.

—LOUIS FINKELSTEIN

Though we do not wholly believe it yet, the interior life is
a real life, and the intangible dreams of people have a tangible
effect on the world.

—JAMES BALDWIN

By "vulgarity," I mean that vice of civilization which makes
man ashamed of himself and his next of kin, and pretend to
be somebody else.

—SOLOMON SCHECHTER

Nor is it always in the most distinguished achievements that
men's virtues or vices may be best discerned; but very often
an action of small note, a short saying, or a jest shall distin-
guish a person's real character more than the greatest sieges
or the most important battles.

—PLUTARCH

It is not external rites that win forgiveness, but inward sin-
cerity.

—TALMUD

A healthy self-regard enables
one to relate well to others...

One's relationship to himself, inner integrity, determines how
he manifests his love to others.

—HASIDIC

The only kind of dignity which is genuine is that which is
not diminished by the indifference of others.

—DAG HAMMARSKJÖLD

At first, a man should himself realize that there are conflict-
situations in his own soul; then he should try to overcome
this inner conflict, so that afterwards he may go out to his
fellow men and enter into new, transformed relations with
them.

—HASIDIC

I need to be aware of myself, in so far as this is also an
awareness of something that goes beyond me as an individual.

—ALBERT CAMUS

Fear always springs from ignorance.

—RALPH WALDO EMERSON

He who gives himself entirely to his fellow-men appears to them useless and selfish; but he who gives himself partially to them is pronounced a benefactor and philanthropist.

—HENRY DAVID THOREAU

Since a man is under obligation to do good himself and make others do good . . . it is therefore not enough that he see to it that he himself walks in upright ways; he must also direct others along the right path. That is why Hillel says, Even when I strive in my own behalf to do the right thing, "what am I?", that is to say, what have I accomplished? Have I fulfilled my obligation? Certainly not—for I must still strive to teach others the right way.

—MIDRASH

Obsession with success, with excelling, indicates an all too familiar neurosis in individual men. The man who is deeply and unshakably sure of himself does not have to be forever proving himself by going one better than his fellows. . . . It must surely be the same with nations, at least with demo-cratic nations.

—EDWARD CRANKSHAW

Why was man created a solitary human being, without a companion? So that it might not be said that some races are better than others.

—TALMUD

Hunger is my native place in the land of the passions. Hunger for fellowship, hunger for righteousness—for a fellowship founded on righteousness, and a righteousness attained in fellowship.

Only life can satisfy the demands of life. And this hunger of mine can be satisfied for the simple reason that the nature of life is such that I can realize my individuality by becoming a bridge for others, a stone in the temple of righteousness.

Don't be afraid of yourself, live your individuality to the full—but for the good of others. Don't copy others in order to buy fellowship, or make convention your law instead of living the righteousness.

To become free and responsible. For this alone was man created, and he who fails to take the Way which could have been his shall be lost eternally.

—DAG HAMMARSKJÖLD

Only if a man knows himself, and has no illusion about himself, and understands every existing thing in relation to itself, will he find real rest [of mind].

—MAIMONIDES

. . . man must strive to recognize the truth and can be fully human only to the extent to which he succeeds in his task. He must be independent and free, an end in himself and not the means for any other person's purposes. He must relate himself to his fellow man lovingly. If he has no love, he is an empty shell even if his were all power, wealth, and intelligence. Man must know the difference between good and evil, he must learn to listen to the voice of his conscience and to be able to follow it.

—ERICH FROMM

First become a blessing to yourself that you may be a blessing to others.

—SAMSON RAPHAEL HIRSCH

If I am for myself alone, what am I...?

All men are made in God's image...

Rabbi Akiba says: Beloved is man, for he was created in God's image. Extraordinary is the love made known to him that he was created in the image of God.

—ETHICS OF THE FATHERS

Are ye not as the children of the Ethiopians unto Me,
O children of Israel? saith the Lord.
Have not I brought up Israel out of the land of Egypt,
And the Philistines from Caphtor,
And Aram from Kir?

—AMOS 9:7

In essence, all human beings are identical. We are all part of One; we are One. This being so, it should not make any difference whom we love. Love should be essentially an act of will, of decision to commit my life completely to that of one other person.

—ERICH FROMM

I am not conscious of a single experience throughout my three months in England and Europe that made me feel that after all East is East and West is West. On the contrary, I have been convinced more than ever that human nature is much the same, no matter under what clime it flourishes, and that if you approached people with trust and affection, you would have ten-fold trust and thousand-fold affection returned to you.

—MAHATMA GANDHI

"That violence whereby sometimes a man doteth upon one creature is but a little spark of that love, even towards all, which lurketh in his nature. When we dote upon the perfections and beauties of some one creature, we do not love that too much, but other things too little. Never was anything in this world loved too much, but many things have been loved in a false way, and all in too short a measure." Traherne might have added (what many poets and novelists have remarked) that, when "we dote upon the perfections and beauties of some one creature," we frequently find ourselves moved to love other creatures. Moreover, to be in love is, in many cases, to have achieved a state of being, in which it becomes possible to have direct intuition of the essentially lovely nature of ultimate reality. "What a world would this be, were everything beloved as it ought to be!" For many people, everything is beloved as it ought to be only when they are in love with "some one creature." The cynical wisdom of the folk affirms that love is blind. But in reality, perhaps, the blind are those who are not in love and who therefore fail to perceive how beautiful the world is and how adorable.

—ALDOUS HUXLEY

See that you do not say, Inasmuch as I have been despised, my fellow shall be despised with me. Rabbi Tanhuma said, If you do this, reflect upon whom you despise: "In the image of God He made him." (Genesis 1:27)

—MIDRASH

. . . it is a small world in the sense of those similarities of trait and tradition that link this planet's inhabitants.

—THEODORE C. SORENSEN

Someone came before Raba and said:
"The mayor of my town has told me:
Go and kill so and so;
if you do not, I will have you killed."
Raba said to him: "Let him kill you, but you must not kill.
What do you think, your blood is redder than another man's?
Perhaps his blood is redder than yours."

—TALMUD

Question: It is written in Proverbs: "As in water face answereth to face, so the heart of man to man." (Proverbs 27:19) Why does the verse read "in water" and not "in a mirror"?

Answer: Man can see his reflection in water only when he bends close to it, and the heart of man too must lean down to the heart of his fellow; then it will see itself within his heart.

—HASIDIC

The one thing in the world, of value, is the active soul. This every man is entitled to; this every man contains within him, although in almost all men obstructed, and as yet unborn. The soul active sees absolute truth and utters truth, or creates. In this action it is genius; not the privilege of here and there a favorite, but the sound estate of every man.

—RALPH WALDO EMERSON

This fourth dimension is universal to all Mankind—it is what makes Man Man. This dimension is the dimension of peace—interior peace.

—EDWARD M. KEATING

A recurrent theme of the early biblical narratives is the rejection of the older brother (whose claim to distinction is based purely on the accident of primogeniture) in favor of the younger brother. This theme is apparent in the accounts of the preference of Isaac over Ishmael, Jacob over Esau, Judah over Reuben, and Ephraim over Manasseh. This can suggest to us that the claim of personal worth is higher than that of prior birth.

—MAX ARZT

All these people [Arameans, Philistines, Ethiopians] and races had a variety of observances and practices which differed with the landscape. But all these peoples and races also were held by the biblical faith to be the children of one God, the father of all men. It would seem inconceivable, if underneath their variety a trace or token of their common origin did not remain. Whatever their differences, the fingerprint of the Creator should be discernible in all His creatures, stamping all as fellow-bearers of the divine image.

—SHALOM SPIEGEL

"God is for man what the sun is for the flowers."
—HEINRICH HEINE

It were wiser to speak less of God, Whom we cannot understand, and more of each other, whom we may understand. Yet I would have you know that we are the breath and the fragrance of God. We are God, in leaf, in flower, and oftentimes in fruit.

—KAHLIL GIBRAN

. . . the doctrine of equality has what as its source? I would say it has religion as its source, it has the Bible as its source. I believe there's no other book which so completely states, and which so completely justifies, the doctrine of equality, where all men are equal because they're all sons of the same father. I think the Bible is the only thing that makes sense: "love thy neighbor as thyself," as the Old Testament keeps on saying over and over and over again. . . .

—MARK VAN DOREN

The highest virtue to which a man can aspire is to become similar to God as far as this is possible: that means that we must imitate His actions by our own, as has been indicated by our Rabbis in their comment on the words "You shall be holy (Leviticus 19:2): As He is gracious, so you be gracious; as He is merciful, so you be merciful."

—MAIMONIDES

Giving oneself to others
opens the way to receive...

The Yehudi was asked: "In the Talmud it says that the stork is called *hasidah* in Hebrew, that is, the devout or the loving one, because he gives so much love to his mate and his young. Then why is he classed in the Scriptures with the unclean birds?"

He answered: "Because he gives love only to his own."

—HASIDIC

We reach out towards the other. In vain—because we have never dared to give ourselves.

—DAG HAMMARSKJÖLD

Why is spontaneous activity the answer to the problem of freedom? . . . Love is the foremost component of such spontaneity; not love as the dissolution of the self in another person, not love as the possession of another person, but love as spontaneous affirmation of others, as the union of the individual with others on the basis of the preservation of the individual self. The dynamic quality of love lies in this very polarity; that it springs from the need of overcoming separateness, that it leads to oneness—and yet that individuality is not eliminated.

—ERICH FROMM

In the Scriptures we read: "I stood between the Lord and you." The "I" stands between God and us.

When a man says "I" and presumes to use his Maker's word, he is shutting himself off from Him. But there is no dividing wall before him who sacrifices his "I." For him it is written: "I am my beloved's, and his desire is toward me." (Song of Songs 7:11) When my "I" comes to belong to my beloved, then his desire is toward me.

—HASIDIC

Thine own friend, and thy father's friend, forsake not;
Neither go into thy brother's house in the day of thy
calamity;
Better is a neighbor that is near than a brother far off.
—PROVERBS 27:10

We should replace our power to destroy with our power to create. We should care about the suffering of human beings—and we should do something about it. We can reach the moon, but we cannot reach across the frontier.

—EDWARD M. KEATING

Divide with reason between self-love and society; and be so true to thyself, as thou be not false to others.

—FRANCIS BACON

It is written: "They saw not one man his brother, neither rose any from his place." (Exodus 10:23) He who will not look at his brother will soon come to this: He will cleave to his place and not be able to move from it.

—HASIDIC

Whoever has it in his power to pray on behalf of his neighbor and fails to do so, is called a sinner; as it is said, "Moreover, as for me, far be it from me, that I should sin against the Lord in ceasing to pray for you." (I Samuel 12:23)

—TALMUD

The Sea of Galilee and the Dead Sea are made of the same water. It flows down, clear and cool, from the heights of Hermon, and the roots of the cedars of Lebanon. The Sea of Galilee makes beauty of it, for the Sea of Galilee has an outlet. It gets to give. It gathers in its riches that it may pour them out again to fertilize the Jordan plain. But the Dead Sea with the same water makes horror. For the Dead Sea has no outlet. It gets to keep.

That is the radical difference between selfish and unselfish men. We all do want life's enriching blessings; we ought to; they are divine benedictions. But some men get to give, and they are like Galilee; while some men get to keep and they are like the brackish water that covers Sodom and Gomorrah.

—ANONYMOUS

A man possesses only what he gives away.

—ELIE WIESEL

Another characteristic of the self-renewing man is that he has mutually fruitful relations with other human beings. He is capable of accepting love and capable of giving it—both more difficult achievements than is commonly thought. He is capable of depending on others and of being depended upon. He can see life through another's eyes and feel it through another's heart.

—JOHN W. GARDNER

Rabbi Yosi said:
All my days I was troubled by this verse:
"And thou shalt grope at noonday, as the blind gropeth in the darkness." (Deuteronomy 28:29)
What difference [I said] to the blind whether it be darkness or light?
Until once I happened upon its meaning.
Once I was walking about in the blackness of night and in

darkness, and saw a blind man walking with a torch in his hand.

I said to him: "My son, why the torch?"

He said to me: "So long as this torch is in my hand, people see me and save me from the pits and thorns and the thistles."

—TALMUD

A minister of modest means lived in a small town, and he was seen driving a Cadillac. Tongues began to wag. One day, the minister came upon a youngster who was admiring the car. As the boy looked up to him, the minister—already sensitive to the talk in town—interpreted the glance of the lad as one of suspicion and accusation.

The minister explained: "I have a rich brother in Texas who sent it to me."

"Boy," said the youngster, "I hope some day I will *be* a brother like that."

—ANONYMOUS

According to the measure that one metes out to others, so is it meted out to him.

—MISHNAH

When one has compassion for others, God has compassion for him.

—TALMUD

Whatever pleases you most in others will infallibly please others in you.

—LORD CHESTERFIELD

There is no room for God in him who is full of himself.

—HASIDIC

Rabbi says, Which is the right course that a man ought to choose for himself? Whatever is deemed praiseworthy by the one who adopts it and for which he is also deemed praiseworthy by men.

—ETHICS OF THE FATHERS

If not now, when...?

And if not now, when? When will the "now" be? The now that is now, the moment in which we are speaking, has never existed from the time when the world was created, and will never again exist. Formerly there was another now, and later there will be another now, and every now has its own particular service. . . .

—HASIDIC

One must not wait for miracles.

—TALMUD

. . . if one advances confidently in the direction of his dreams, and endeavors to live the life which he has imagined, he will meet with a success unexpected in common hours. . . . If you have built castles in the air, your work need not be lost; that is where they should be. Now put the foundations under them.

—HENRY DAVID THOREAU

Knowledge may give weight, but accomplishments only give lustre; and many more people see than weigh.

—LORD CHESTERFIELD

A man should have no purpose in the learning of wisdom
save only this—to learn to know wisdom itself. Similarly, no
purpose must be connected with truth, save that one should
know what is true. And . . . to live by it.

—MAIMONIDES

Accustom yourself to complete any good work you have
undertaken.

—TALMUD

If the world is not to sink under its own burden . . . strength,
force, astuteness and similar virtues, desirable in themselves
as manifestations of vigorous manhood but dangerously bor-
dering on violence and brutality, will be less valued than
meekness, gentleness, sweetness of disposition and humility. It
will not be the strong man, but the good man, the affectionate
man, who will form the desired goal of parents and peda-
gogues.

Organization itself, this great achievement of our age, will
largely give way to generous impulses and broad sympathies.
I by no means underrate the value and importance of organization. It certainly turns mobs into societies and societies
into powerful units. It is for the adult what method and system are for the young in the school. But it can be decidedly
overdone, and if not under the control of a strong moral
principle, touched by kindness and goodness, modifying the
severity and its tendency to inconsiderateness, it is more likely
to further passion than compassion. The same is true of effi-
ciency, which has constantly to be qualified by fitness.

—SOLOMON SCHECHTER

Go to, boy. The world is yours. Nothing is done, nothing is
known. The greatest poem isn't written, the best railroad isn't
built yet, the perfect state hasn't been thought of. Everything remains to be done—right, everything.

—EVELYN NIXON

Whatsoever thy hand attaineth to do by thy strength, that do; for there is no work, nor device, nor knowledge, nor wisdom in the grave, whither thou goest.

—ECCLESIASTES 9:10

The biggest lesson of all to be learned about contemporary civilization is that nothing anyone is doing today makes any sense unless it is connected to the making of a genuine peace.

—NORMAN COUSINS

. . . if we cannot end now our differences, at least we can help make the world safe for diversity. For, in the final analysis, our most basic common link is that we all inhabit this small planet. We all breathe the same air. We all cherish our children's future. And we are all mortal.

—JOHN F. KENNEDY

Man must be able to give all his tomorrows for today so that he should not have to spend all his todays for one tomorrow.

—RABBI YOIZEL

Said the Kotzker Rabbi: There are three ways in which a man can go about performing a good deed. If he says: "I shall do it soon," the way is poor. If he says: "I am ready to do it now," the way is of average quality. If he says: "I am doing it," the way is praiseworthy.

—HASIDIC

One of our greatest needs is persons who can aid in the process of social healing.

—ARTHUR G. COONS

Today the colleges and universities . . . and the public school systems . . . are the means of clearing the way to the future . . .

Edmund Burke, one of England's greatest statesmen, spoke with prophetic wisdom when he said: "The public interest requires doing today the things that men of intelligence and good will would wish, five or ten years hence, had been done."

—DAVID SARNOFF

That word, security, represents the end upon which the hearts of men and women everywhere today are set. Whether it be security from bombing from the air, or from mass destruction; whether it be security from want, disease, and starvation; whether it be security in enjoying that inalienable right which every human being should possess of living out his life in peace and happiness, people throughout the length and breadth of the world are demanding security and freedom from fear.

That is the objective before us all today—to try and find a means of bringing that to pass.

—SUMNER WELLES

When an opportunity to do a good deed presents itself, do not put it off saying, in effect, "I will wait for a greater opportunity."

—MIDRASH

7. THE MISTAKE

The Mistake . . .

It is a common mistake—indeed, the mistake of mistakes—
to imagine we can influence anyone else to take the path
of goodness, unless and until we travel it ourselves.

Do you want a good family?
. . . a better community?
. . . a greater nation?
We all say we do.

And who doesn't *know* the directions in which we would
like to see his family, his community, his nation improve.

But to *know* the difference between what is good and bad
is not enough.

And to *call on others* to do what is right is not enough.

Out of a deep and important impulse, we often want
those around us to behave even better than we do;
setting higher standards for our children, and our neighbors, than we achieve for ourselves.

We urge *them* to be better—and it is good to want them
to be so.

But this is never enough.

The mistake of mistakes is to imagine we can influence
anyone else to take the path of goodness, *unless and until
we travel it ourselves.*

A Good Family . . .

The good family is one whose members find both strength
and enjoyment in each other.

But there is no doubt that the complexities and uncertainties of our life in our time make it harder for almost any family to stay together, share together, develop together.

How, then, can we best cope with the forces which tend to diffuse family life today?

We must begin by understanding how much we must give of *ourselves* to the task: of our time, our energies, our patience—even as we do in any other area of life where we want to achieve success.

For while a family is given to everyone, a *good* family is something *we must create.*

This is a never-ending process, as the family keeps growing and changing. Unique problems arise out of the uneasiness of each member of the family. And, being human, we are bound to make mistakes.

Yet, while recognizing that mistakes *are* inevitable, we can also know that almost no mistake is *final*. Always, we have the opportunity to learn and advance and grow from our mistakes.

Above all, we must realize that *our own behavior* is the primary creative force in the development of our family.

If we want a child to listen to us, we must learn to listen to him.

If husband and wife want more concern and understanding from each other, each must show greater understanding for the other's problems.

If we want our family to follow the wisdom of our tradition, we must truly try to live by this wisdom ourselves.

The mistake of mistakes is to imagine there is any other way to create a good family than by the example we set *by the continuing testimony of our daily acts.*

A Better Community . . .

To build a better community, we must move in two directions at the same time:

> Increasingly, to give every man, woman and child greater opportunities and encouragement to develop what is best in himself.

> Increasingly, to get all to understand that their security can be ultimately assured only by the security and welfare of everyone else.

This has been true throughout history—even in much smaller, simpler societies, whose people had the same origins, same traditions, same ways of life. And it is just as true today, in our swiftly growing communities, where many millions of people of different origins, different traditions, different ways of life now live and work together.

Such differences may sometimes make it difficult to see how much we *are* all neighbors to one another.

Yet we are.

And we cannot forget that a neighbor is someone for whom we should have the concerns and understanding and love we want for ourselves.

Moreover, without accepting the obligations of being a good neighbor, *we cannot hope to achieve a better community* for our children.

That is why for us to *talk* about the problems of our community—of better housing, of improved education, of higher standards of morality, of increased beauty—is not enough.

We must, instead, directly involve ourselves: giving of *our* time and energies to the task of bettering our community.

The mistake of mistakes is to imagine we can achieve a better community by calling on others to do more than *we are ready to do ourselves.*

A Greater Nation . . .

How do we measure the greatness of a nation?

We have lived to see our nation rise to leadership as world spokesman for the fundamental liberties of man: his rights to self-government, his equality before the law, the human dignities of freedom of religion, of reason, of responsibility.

Certainly, it is by these ancient-rooted values of the American tradition that we measure our greatness—far more than by any physical power and wealth.

It is, therefore, not enough for us to help and protect other nations out of our great material resources. It is not enough for us to relieve the hungry and support the weak. We can fulfill the obligations of our leadership only by helping the people of the world to develop their own liberties.

But we can only become such a true leader of nations by *being* a greater nation—by the demonstration of how *we* live up to our own best concepts of individual freedom and mutual responsibility, both at home and abroad.

The mistake of mistakes is to imagine we can hope to influence other nations and people to do what is right, *unless and until they see us do what is right.*

Each of us is part of a family
. . . a community
. . . a nation.

And we all want to increase the goodness of our family, our community, our nation.

To do so surely requires all the wisdom we can garner and share with others.

It surely demands all the concern we can generate and communicate.

But finally—beyond wisdom and beyond concern—there must be the eloquence of our own right behavior.

"If one's wisdom exceeds onc's deeds, the wisdom will not endure." (Ethics of the Fathers 3:12)

No mistake is final...

The angels have their virtues and flaws, and men have their virtues and flaws. The virtue of angels is that they cannot deteriorate, and their flaw is that they cannot improve. Man's flaw is that he can deteriorate, and his virtue that he can improve.

—HASIDIC

Which is the perfect repentance? When an occasion arises for repeating a transgression once committed, and it is in the sinner's power to sin again, but he makes himself free, and does not do it.

—MAIMONIDES

It is not, in fact, in the nature of human beings to be perfectly accurate, and it is unrealistic to believe they ever will be. The only reasonable way to get a program right is to assume that it will at first contain errors and take steps to discover these and correct them.

—CHRISTOPHER STRACHEY

When one knows of what man is capable, for better and for worse, one also knows that it is not the human being himself who must be protected but the possibilities he has within him —in other words, his freedom. . . .

Freedom is nothing else but a chance to be better, whereas enslavement is a certainty of the worst.

—ALBERT CAMUS

. . . repentance is not remorse for the past but a serious attempt to profit in the future by the lessons of the past. . . . No ailment of the soul . . . is worse than discouragement; man must again and again renew the idea of courage in his mind. He must not become discouraged if he fails to observe any improvement in his moral qualities, after long labor of self-discipline. He should know that his work was not in vain but has left its beneficial effects which, though invisible at the moment, will become visible in time. Drops of water continually falling upon a rock will finally wear it away though the first drops seem to produce no effect at all. It is the same with self-discipline; its effects cannot fail to penetrate our hearts if we practice it continually.

—LOUIS GINZBERG

On the whole, I think we shall survive. The outlook is as bad as it has ever been, but thinking people realize that—and therein lies the hope of its getting better.

—JAWAHARLAL NEHRU

I believe that we must try to overcome this excessive moralism, which binds us to old myths and blinds us to new realities and, worse still, leads us to regard new and unfamiliar ideas with fear and mistrust.

—J. WILLIAM FULBRIGHT

This is a story about Rabbi Simeon, son of Eliezar, who was returning from Migdal-Eder, from the house of his master. He rode on a donkey, ambling along the seashore in a leisurely fashion. There he came upon a man who was exceedingly ugly to look upon. He said to him: "Amazing how ugly the children of our father Abraham can be!"

Said the other to him: "What shall I do? Tell it to the artist who made me."

Immediately Rabbi Simeon, son of Eliezer, got down from his donkey, prostrated himself before the other, and said: "I bow down to you; forgive me!"

Said the other to him: "I cannot forgive you until you go to the artist who made me, and say to him: 'How ugly is this implement you have made!' "

But the rabbi walked after him for half a mile. Then the people of the town heard of it, went forth to meet him, and said to him: "Peace be with you, master!"

Said the ugly one to them: "Whom do you address as master?"

Said they to him: "Him who is walking behind you."

Said he to them: "If that is a master, may there not be many like him in Israel!"

Said they to him: "God forfend! What has he done to you?"

And he told them the whole matter. And they urged him greatly to forgive. He said: "Very well, I forgive him, provided he does not make a habit of saying such things."

—TALMUD

Man is the only creature endowed with conscience. His conscience is the voice which calls him back to himself, it permits him to know what he ought to do in order to become himself, it helps him to remain aware of the aims of his life and of the norms necessary for the attainment of these aims. We are therefore not helpless victims of circumstance; we are, indeed, able to change and to influence forces inside and outside ourselves and to control, at least to some extent, the conditions which play upon us.

—ERICH FROMM

The Hebrew language has no exact equivalent for the term New Year. "Rosh Hashanah" means literally, the beginning of the year. In a sense, the year is not new. Not the year, but each individual must become as new.

—MAX ARZT

> Before the mountains were brought
>   forth,
> Or ever Thou hadst formed the earth
>   and the world,
> Even from everlasting to everlasting,
>   Thou art God.
> Thou turnest man to contrition:
> And sayest: "Return, ye children of men."

—PSALMS 90:2-3

Man is like a rooster entangled in flax, who must rest on one leg to extricate the other leg. He must break away from one bad habit, leaving another on which to stand.

—RABBI YOIZEL

> In the school of affliction I have learned more philosophy than at the academy, and more divinity than from the pulpit.

—DANIEL DEFOE

Transgressions between man and man—that is, if one injured, cursed or robbed his neighbor—are not forgiven until the offender compensates his victim and begs his forgiveness. Although the monies were returned, he must still pacify him, and beseech his forgiveness. If he has hurt his neighbor with words only, he must pacify him and implore him, until he grants forgiveness.

However, if his neighbor refuses to forgive, let him send three men from among his friends to urge him and to plead with him. And if he still refuses, a second and third group of three must be sent. If his neighbor persists in his obduracy,

he shall leave him and go his way. In such circumstances,
he who refuses to forgive becomes the sinner.

Yet if a man has transgressed against his teacher, he must
come and go, and come and go, even a thousand times, until
he obtains forgiveness.

—MAIMONIDES

Nought is given 'neath the sun,
Nought is had that is not won.
—SWEDISH HYMN

Not the saint, but the sinner that repenteth, is he to whom
the full length and breadth, and height and depth, of life's
meaning is revealed. Not the absence of vice, but vice there,
and virtue holding her by the throat, seems the ideal human
state.

—WILLIAM JAMES

I have not the shadow of a doubt that any man or woman
can achieve what I have if he or she would make the same
effort and cultivate the same hope and faith. I am but a poor
struggling soul yearning to be wholly good . . . I know that I
have still before me a difficult path to traverse.

—MAHATMA GANDHI

. . . I have necessarily to do with that problematic type . . .
life has become baseless for him. He cannot tread on firm
soil, on firm earth. He is, so to speak, suspended in the air.
And what does he want? . . . a being not only whom he can
trust as a man trusts another, but a being that gives him now
the certitude that "there is a soil, there *is* an existence. The
world is not condemned to deprivation, degeneration, destruction. The world *can* be redeemed. *I* can be redeemed
because there is this trust." And if this is reached, now I
can help this man even in his struggle against himself.

—MARTIN BUBER

Their ways are always before him;
They cannot be hidden from his eyes. . . .
All their doings are as clear as the sun before him,
And his eyes rest continually upon their ways.
Their iniquities are not hidden from him,
And all their sins are before the Lord. . . .
Afterward he will rise up and requite them,
And pay back their recompense upon their heads.
But to those who repent he has given a way to return,
And he encourages those whose endurance fails.

—ECCLESIASTICUS 17:15–16, 19–21, 23–24

The power of an individual's example...

Where there are no men, strive to be a man.
                    —ETHICS OF THE FATHERS

This is what Rabbi Leib, son of Sarah, used to say about those rabbis who expounded the Torah:

"What does it amount to—their expounding the Torah? A man should see to it that all his actions are a Torah and that he himself becomes so entirely a Torah that one can learn from his habits and his motions and his motionless clinging to God."

                    —HASIDIC

God never appears to you in person but in action.
                    —MAHATMA GANDHI

If there is any one characteristic which distinguishes the older generation, it is this belief that social ills may be cured by personal virtue. Its highest moral ideals are sacrifice and service.

                    —RANDOLPH BOURNE

There are pretenders to devotion as to courage; and even as those who are truly brave when honor calls are not those who make the most noise, so the good and truly pious, in whose footsteps we ought to follow, are not those who make so many grimaces.

—MOLIÈRE

Like Rabbi Akiba, or Mar Samuel, the Gaon [of Vilna] became influential among his contemporaries only by his teaching and his exemplary life.

—SOLOMON SCHECHTER

Inspiration is linked to aspiration. If men have learned how to get along with other people, how indeed to draw forth from their fellows the sense of confidence, if they have learned something of what really constitutes personal integrity, they are more worthy for responsible positions of leadership.

—ARTHUR G. COONS

"And thou shalt love the Lord thy God." (Deuteronomy 6:5) This means that one should act in such a manner that the name of God shall be beloved by others . . . that one's business can be carried on honestly and other relations with people in a proper and commendable manner, so that people might say: "Happy is his father who taught him Torah; happy is his teacher who taught him Torah, for see him who has studied, how exemplary is his conduct."

—TALMUD

That mercy I to others show,
That mercy show to me.

—ALEXANDER POPE

The fact that, in the language of the Rabbis, the term for studying the Law and discussing it is "to attend" or rather "to serve the disciples of the Wise" may also have led people to the important truth that the great man is not a lecturing machine, but a sort of living Law himself. "When the man," said one Rabbi, "has wholly devoted himself to the Torah, and thoroughly identified himself with it, it becomes almost his own Torah." Thus people have not only to listen to his words but to observe his whole life, and to profit from all his actions and movements.

—SOLOMON SCHECHTER

> This lament for a golden age is only a lament for golden men.
>
> —HENRY DAVID THOREAU

The heart of man will in all ages retain idealism enough to love and revere the greatest of men and to follow what was best in them.

—SOLOMON SCHECHTER

> . . . a man of rare moral depth, warmth or delicacy may be a more important element in the advance of civilization than the newest and truest idea derived from the fundamental principles of the science of morals. . . . What most appeals to our imagination and sympathy in history is heroism, and saintliness is only another word for heroism in the domain of ethics and religion.
>
> —LOUIS GINZBERG

People say that the art of printing has brought us great advantages, whereas it has in fact been detrimental to us. For in former days authors were handsomely paid, and people would buy from them only the good, pleasing, useful books, while the useless vain books would of themselves disappear.

Not so, however, in our days, when many ignorant people assume airs, and, though benighted and smaller than the least throughout their lives, seek to set themselves up as shining lights to another generation that has not learned to know them. And everyone who possibly can, and whose wealth is greater than his understanding, connives to publish books in which he is arbitrarily referred to as a great and worthy man, whereas he is no more an authority than is a carpenter's apprentice.

—JOSEPH SOLOMON DEL MEGIDO

A little knowledge that *acts* is worth infinitely more than much knowledge that is idle.

—KAHLIL GIBRAN

What *is* the sort of thinking we shall have to do? It is the thinking necessary to the good citizen, the good neighbor, the good father or mother of a family, the competent man of affairs, the supporter of sound causes generally, the person with sensitive allergies for political hocum, specious advertising, religious superstition, class and race tension, and lopsided partisanship in all its fifty-seven varieties.

—BRAND BLANSHARD

Individual Americans—truck drivers and editors, grocers and senators, beauty operators and ball players—can contribute to the greatness and strength of a free society, or they can help it to die.

—JOHN W. GARDNER

"*Do not do to others what you would not have them do to you*" is one of the most fundamental principles of ethics. But it is equally justifiable to state: *Whatever you do to others, you also do to yourself.*

—ERICH FROMM

Aaron had a habit of associating with evil people until they grew embarrassed and thought, "Woe unto us! If Aaron knew what we are like, what our life is like, he would resolve never again to set eye upon us. He must think we are worthy people. We ought at least to try to make our conduct correspond to his thinking." In that way they would be drawn to association with him and learning Torah from him.

—MEIRI

Improve yourself before you attempt to improve others.

—TALMUD

God said to Moses: Is there respect of persons with me? Whether it be Israelite or Gentile, man or woman, slave or handmaid, whoso doeth a good deed, shall find the reward at its side, as it is written: "Thy righteousness is like the everlasting hills . . . man and beast alike Thou savest, O Lord." (Psalms 36:7)

—MIDRASH

The power of a nation's example...

A member of a church, at a reception, closed his remarks with the pious hope "that the Lord is on our side." "I am not at all concerned about that," commented the President [Lincoln], "for we know that the Lord is always on the side of right. But it is my constant anxiety and prayer that I and the nation should be on the Lord's side."

—SOLOMON SCHECHTER

There are those, I know, who will reply that the liberation of humanity, the freedom of man and mind, is nothing but a dream. They are right. It is. It is the American dream.

—ARCHIBALD MACLEISH

. . . God was very good to this country in terms of raw material. But we haven't got a thing that isn't matched elsewhere in the world.

No, it is something in the hearts of men. It is a spiritual quality in the American people that is the very essence of our way of life. In this system of free enterprise we rely upon rewarding the individual in proportion to his effort and surrounding him with a congenial atmosphere in which to work so that each man in our great country works with joy in his heart and hope in the future.

—CLARENCE B. RANDALL

Living in the big house on the top of the hill has always carried with it liabilities, problems, responsibilities.

No amount of material aid we give will make for genuine friendship unless we also give respect and the things that go with respect.

In short, the human decencies come first.

—NORMAN COUSINS

The seventy sacrifices brought in the Temple during the festival of Succoth were [in petition] for the welfare of the nations of the world, that they should continue to exist.

—MIDRASH

. . . the real America, all stumblings and aberrations notwithstanding, is an upright society of self-respecting human beings banded together in mutual support against the elemental forces, against tyrants, against everything that threatens the free development of individual decency, freedom and responsibility. . . .

—EDWARD CRANKSHAW

With the supermarket as our temple and the singing commercial as our litany, are we likely to fire the world with an irresistible vision of America's exalted purposes and inspiring way of life?

—ADLAI E. STEVENSON

Changing an economy means in fact changing a whole generation of men. I doubt if that can be done in less than two decades. So I would say: Look on the fateful program of modernizing what the French call the "third world"—the world of the poor and dispossessed—as on the program for probing the planets. Expect failures. Rejoice in successes. Never doubt the job can be done. Indeed it must be done if misery is not to turn to despair, despair to wars, and war to ruin for us all.

But it must also be done because of a much profounder reason: for it is wrong to leave children to starve who could eat with our help, wrong to let youngsters die when medical skill can save them, wrong to leave men and women without shelter, wrong to accept for others, in the midst of our own abundance, the iron pains of degrading want.

—ADLAI E. STEVENSON

For the American idea, quite literally and realistically, *is* America. If we had not held these truths to be self-evident, if we had not believed that all men are created equal, if we had not believed that they are endowed, all of them with certain inalienable rights, we should never have become America, whatever else we might have become.

—ARCHIBALD MACLEISH

Come, I will make the continent indissoluble,
I will make the most splendid race
    the sun ever shone upon,
I will make divine magnetic lands,
  With the love of comrades,
    With the life-long love of comrades.
I will plant companionship thick as trees along all the rivers
    of America, and along the shores of the great lakes and
    all over the prairies,
I will make inseparable cities with their arms about each
    other's necks,
  By the love of comrades,
    By the manly love of comrades.
For you these from me, O Democracy,
    to serve you ma femme!
For you, for you I am trilling these
    songs.

—WALT WHITMAN

Within its population of slightly less than one hundred and thirty million, the United States has today over thirty million citizens—the overwhelming majority of them young citizens —who are the American-born children of immigrant parents of various nationalities: German, Italian, Polish, Czech, Slovak, Serbian, Croatian, Slovenian, Bulgarian, Jewish, Russian, Carpatho-Russian, Ukranian, Lithuanian, Finnish, Hungarian, Norwegian, Swedish, Danish, Dutch, French, Flemish, Spanish, Portuguese, Rumanian, Armenian, Syrian, Lett, Albanian, Greek, Turkish, and, of course, English, Scotch, and Irish.

—LOUIS ADAMIC

On that day shall Israel be the third with Egypt and with Assyria, a blessing in the midst of the earth; for that the Lord of hosts hath blessed him, saying: "Blessed be Egypt My people and Assyria the work of My hands, and Israel Mine inheritance."

—ISAIAH 19:24–25

Let us restore to social intercourse that harmony and affection without which liberty and even life itself are but dreary things. And let us reflect that having banished from our land that religious intolerance under which mankind so long bled and suffered, we have yet gained a little if we countenance a political intolerance as despotic, as wicked, and capable of as bitter and bloody persecutions.

—THOMAS JEFFERSON

Nations have been wrecked because they lacked an overriding moral goal to which individuals could commit themselves. History shows us that when we become success-dominated, we lose sight of our real reasons for living.

—LOUIS FINKELSTEIN

The United States was the first nation in the world to provide schools for all children, and that is one reason we have prospered. If our schools fail, it will not be because we care too much for our ideals but because we care too little.

—SLOAN WILSON

Hear the words of the Lord,
Ye rulers of Sodom;
Give ear unto the law of our God,
Ye people of Gomorrah.
To what purpose is the multitude
    of your sacrifices unto Me?
Saith the Lord . . .
Wash you, make you clean,
Put away the evil of your doings
From before Mine eyes,
Cease to do evil;
Learn to do well;
Seek justice, relieve the oppressed,
Judge the fatherless, plead for the widow.
               —ISAIAH 1:10–11, 16–17

> The democratic values of Western civilization must exclude
> parochialism, must include a readiness not so much to proselytize as to share.
>
>   —PHILIP C. JESSUP

. . . if there is anything which is characteristic of this country
it is its tendency toward corporate endeavor, its ability to
merge the narrow and sluggish rivulets of individual energy
into the broad and swift current of a corporation or society.
"When an American has an idea," quoth a famous French
writer, "he directly seeks a second American to share it. If
there be three, they elect a president and two secretaries.
Given four, they name a keeper of records and the office is
ready for work; five, they convene a general meeting and the
society is fully constituted."
               —ISRAEL FRIEDLAENDER

> Righteousness exalteth a nation;
> But sin is a reproach to any people.
>   —PROVERBS 14:34

"We are not enemies, but friends. We must not be enemies. Though passion may have strained, it must not break our bonds of affection. The mystic cords of memory, stretching from every battlefield and patriot grave to every living heart and hearthstone over all this broad land, will yet swell the chorus of the Union when again touched, as surely they will be, by the better angels of our nature." . . . The expression, "mystic chords of memory," is significant. Napoleon the Great is recorded to have once made the apt remark, "Religion means memory." If the Union was to be saved, it had to be raised to the dignity of a religion, which means memory, an object hallowed by past associations, which alone holds our promises for the future. . . .

A certain Jewish saint who had the misfortune to survive the death of his greatest disciple, is recorded to have exclaimed: "O Lord, Thou shouldst be grateful to me that I have trained for Thee so noble a soul." This is somewhat too bold, but we may be grateful to God for having given us such a great soul as Lincoln, "who, under God, gave this nation a new birth of freedom," and to our dear country, which by its institutions and its people rendered possible the greatness for which Abraham Lincoln shall stand forever.

—SOLOMON SCHECHTER

Glossary

BEN   Hebrew word meaning "son."

HASIDIC   Hasidism is a religious movement founded by Israel Baal Shem Tov in eastern Europe in the eighteenth century. Hasidic rabbis, known as Tzadikim ("righteous ones"), are the source of instruction and inspiration for their followers, known as Hasidim ("pious ones"). Hasidic teaching stresses personal piety, soundness of individual behavior and the joy of religious experience. The ideas and values of the movement are often expressed in stories, allegories and aphorisms.

IBN   Arabic word meaning "son."

MIDRASH   ("Exposition," "Inquiry"): The exegesis of scripture by the rabbis of the Talmudic period (see below) and several centuries thereafter. It is applied mainly to the nonlegal interpretation of scripture such as legends, folklore, moral sayings and ethical insights. Volumes of Midrash are frequently named according to the book of the Bible under discussion. Midrash Rabbah ("Great Midrash") consists of ten books, one for each volume of the Pentateuch (Genesis, Exodus, Leviticus Numbers, Deuteronomy) and one for each of the five scrolls (Song of Songs, Ruth, Lamentations, Ecclesiastes, Esther). The names of several other volumes of Midrash are: Mehilta, Sifre, Sifra, Pesikta de Rav Kahana, Tanna debe Eliyahu, Tanhuma.

MISHNAH   ("Repetition," "Studying"): The code of law based on the discussions and discourses of rabbis and sages over many centuries. It was compiled, systematized and recorded by Rabbi Judah ha-Nasi ("the prince") at the end of the second century. It has six major divisions. The subject matter includes religious law, civil and criminal law, standards of conduct, ethical principles. A popular tractate of Mishnah is Pirke Avoth (Chapters or Ethics of the Fathers). The Fathers According to Rabbi Nathan (not part of the Mishnah) is a commentary and further elaboration of the Ethics of the Fathers.

TALMUD   ("Teaching"): The two parts of Talmud are the Mishnah (see above) and the Gemara ("study"). The latter is the discussion and further elaboration of the law as recorded in the Mishnah. The Babylonian Talmud records the discussion of the Bible in the academies of that land from the years 200–500 C.E. The Jerusalem (or Palestinian) Talmud derives from the discussion in the academies of that country from the years 200–400 C.E.

TORAH   ("Instruction"): The first five books of scripture: Genesis, Exodus, Leviticus, Numbers and Deuteronomy. However, the origin of the word ("to instruct," "to guide") reflects the broader meaning of Torah. The traditions of Judaism, its literature, instruction in the broadest sense, are identified as Torah. It is also translated as The Law, deriving from the laws of justice and mercy which are basic to Torah.

ZOHAR   (Sefer ha-Zohar, "Book of Splendor"): The basic volumes of Jewish mysticism, written as a commentary principally on the Pentateuch. Traditionally, its authorship has been accredited to Rabbi Simeon ben Yohai (circa second century) but is now attributed to Moses de Leon, a thirteenth-century Spanish Kabbalist (Jewish mystic). Subsequent Jewish mysticism is based on this volume.

Index to Sources

The page numbers in italics cited herein refer to pages in this book, not to the original source. Where two quotations from the same source appear on one page, the first reference is marked 1, *the second* 2.

ABOUT THE AUTHOR

RABBI BERNARD MANDELBAUM is President of The Jewish Theological Seminary of America and Seminary Professor of Homiletics and Reader in Midrash on the faculty of the Rabbinical Department. Dr. Mandelbaum was Provost of the Seminary from 1961 to 1966, and from 1951 to 1961 he was Dean of Students at the Seminary's Rabbinical School. He has also served as program editor of the Seminary's *Eternal Light* radio and television series. One of the *Eternal Light* dramas won a Sylvania TV award and another was nominated for an Emmy Award.

Dr. Mandelbaum has written many articles, both scholarly and popular, on the ethics and on the interpretation of Judaism. He edited *Assignment in Israel*, a collection of essays published in 1960. His critical edition of the Pesikta (a rabbinic commentary on parts of Scripture) appeared in 1962. Dr. Mandelbaum is presently preparing a critical edition of the Midrash Tanchuma and is working on a volume of the writings of Solomon Schechter, the Jewish scholar.

A native New Yorker, Dr. Mandelbaum is married to the former Judith Werber and is the father of five children.